Using your
Computer
The **beginner's** guide
Third Edition

© Haynes Publishing 2003
Reprinted 2004
Second edition published 2006
Third edition published 2011

All rights reserved. No part of this publication may be reproduced or
stored in a retrieval system or transmitted, in any form or by any means,
electronic, mechanical, photocopying, recording or otherwise, without
prior permission in writing from the publisher.

Published by: Haynes Publishing
Sparkford, Yeovil, Somerset BA22 7JJ
Tel: 01963 442030 Fax: 01963 440001
Int. tel: +44 1963 442030 Fax: +44 1963 440001
E-mail: sales@haynes.co.uk
Website: www.haynes.co.uk

British Library Cataloguing in Publication Data:
A catalogue record for this book is available from the British Library

ISBN 978 0 85733 120 5

Printed and bound in the USA by Odcombe Press LP,
1299 Bridgestone Parkway, La Vergne, TN 37086

Throughout this book, trademarked names are used. Rather than put a
trademark symbol after every occurrence of a trademarked name, we use
the names in an editorial fashion only, and to the benefit of the trademark
owner, with no intention of infringement of the trademark. Where such
designations appear in this book, they have been printed with initial caps.

Whilst we at J. H. Haynes & Co. Ltd strive to ensure the accuracy and
completeness of the information in this manual, it is provided entirely at
the risk of the user. Neither the company nor the author can accept liability
for any errors, omissions or damage resulting therefrom. In particular,
users should be aware that component and accessory manufacturers,
and software providers, can change specifications without notice, thus
appropriate professional advice should always be sought.

Using your
Computer

The beginner's guide

Third Edition

Kyle MacRae

For PCs running **Windows 7** Home Premium

Contents

Introduction

So you've finally taken the plunge and bought yourself a PC – or perhaps had one foisted upon you by an impatient offspring? Well, congratulations! May we say that you couldn't have picked a better time for it. Relatively speaking, today's personal computer is cheaper, smarter and vastly more powerful than those of yesteryear … but that's all by the by. What matters more in the present context is that it's much easier to get to grips with a computer than ever before.

It's getting better all the time

For all its many marvels, the average personal computer has long been over-complicated, counter-intuitive and prone to doing the dumbest things at times. However, the introduction of Windows 7, particularly the Home Premium version which we'll be looking at here, has gone a long way towards bridging the gap between

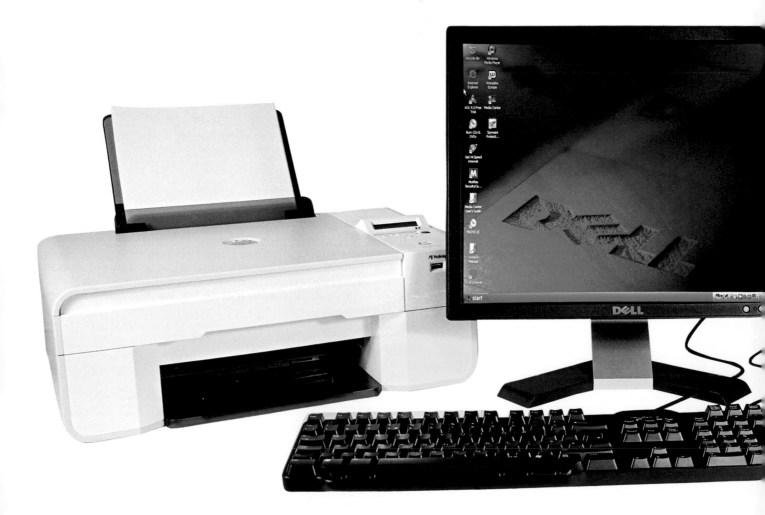

a computer's capability and its usability. More often than not, you will discover that your PC will 'just work' – and that's a remarkable step forward in computer evolution.

The real keys to understanding your new machine are taking things slowly and keeping it simple. This is why you won't find us pointing out ten different ways to do everything. Rather, we'll concentrate exclusively on the absolute essentials and tackle each new subject in jargon-free plain English.

In time, you will doubtless want to learn more about your computer and what it can do for you. We would certainly encourage this: invoke the help of friends or colleagues, undertake a course in computing, or just spend a little time experimenting. But our present aim, while modest, is giving you the know-how you need to begin using your computer.

We will assume from the outset that you know next to, or absolutely, nothing about computers. Much of what follows will therefore appear trivial to those with some practical experience under their belts. But they can look elsewhere. This is unashamedly a manual for the complete beginner.

A personal note

I once worked as a computer consultant, helping newcomers to buy, set up and use their first PC. One afternoon, I found myself plugging together a client's brand new state-of-the-art computer system – an exuberant and ill-advised (though not by me) purchase which had set him back some ludicrous sum. When all was ready, I handed over the reins – well, the mouse – and proclaimed: 'OK, click the Start button and let's get going!'

Some 40 minutes later (I kid you not), we were still sat at that desk, trying repeatedly, desperately but ultimately unsuccessfully to make that click. For the avoidance of doubt, this client was a retired professional with dextrous hands, perfectly good eyesight and the full complement of faculties. But he just could not relate the movements of a slithery lump of plastic on a rubber mat to those of a pointer on his PC's monitor screen. I shared his frustration as the pointer darted around the screen from corner to corner, beyond his control and beyond his ken; and I may even have echoed his soft curse when finally the pointer came close enough to the Start button to hazard a speculative click … only for the mouse to wobble in his hand and send the pointer skating across the screen once more.

It struck me then, as it strikes me now, that there is a pressing need for a practical guide that makes no assumptions whatsoever about the relationship between a computer and its owner. A mouse is not an intuitive way to control a computer, any more than pressing a pedal is an intuitive way to make a car go faster, or stop; these things have to be taught, learned and practised, not taken for granted and glossed over.

This, then, is the book written for the frustrated 'newbie' who really wants to use a computer but isn't quite sure where to start … and doesn't fancy taking a degree in geekology just to be able to send an e-mail.

How to use this book

For the sake of consistency and clarity, we will use certain conventions throughout this manual.

Mouse instructions

When you see the  symbol, we are referring to an action performed with the mouse. So, for instance,

> Start

means 'use the mouse to move the on-screen pointer to the Start button, and click it'.

Furthermore, most mouse-driven actions involve several steps. Each step starts on a new line. As a rule, when we say 'click', we mean click the left mouse button once.
Don't worry – this will become clear soon enough.

There are two other mouse actions, double click and right button click. All three actions appear as follows;

> *Single click on the left mouse button*

> *Double click on the left mouse button*

> *Single click on the right mouse button*

Screen examples

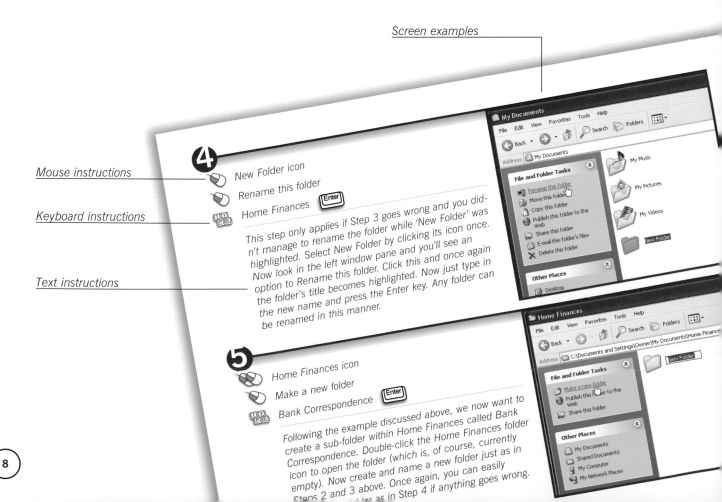

Mouse instructions

Keyboard instructions

Text instructions

4
New Folder icon
Rename this folder
Home Finances [Enter]

This step only applies if Step 3 goes wrong and you did-n't manage to rename the folder while 'New Folder' was highlighted. Select New Folder by clicking its icon once. Now look in the left window pane and you'll see an option to Rename this folder. Click this and once again the folder's title becomes highlighted. Now just type in the new name and press the Enter key. Any folder can be renamed in this manner.

5
Home Finances icon
Make a new folder
Bank Correspondence [Enter]

Following the example discussed above, we now want to create a sub-folder within Home Finances called Bank Correspondence. Double-click the Home Finances folder icon to open the folder (which is, of course, currently empty). Now create and name a new folder just as in Steps 2 and 3 above. Once again, you can easily ... as in Step 4 if anything goes wrong.

Keyboard instructions

When you see the symbol, the directions refer to the keyboard. For example:

 *teapot*

means 'type the word "teapot" on the keyboard now'. Type exactly what you see, being sure to note any spaces or unusual symbols.

However, when the direction is contained within square brackets, this indicates that you should type something that pertains to you specifically e.g.

 *[your e-mail address]*

means 'type in your own e-mail address'. We'll soon have you using the keyboard with abandon.

When we want you to press a certain key on the keyboard, this is denoted by means of a box. Thus

[Enter]

means 'press the Enter key'.

Where an action requires you to press more than one key simultaneously, we use the + symbol to link them. Thus

[Ctrl] + [Alt] + [Delete]

is an instruction to press the three named keys at the same time. And it really doesn't get any more complicated than that!

Text instructions

Beneath the mouse and keyboard directions, we explain the purpose and method of each step in more detail. Please read these instructions in full before clicking the mouse or typing on the keyboard.

Jargon

Any word or phrase highlighted like *this* is fully explained in the glossary. This helps to keep the main text clear of non-essential clutter. To avoid an over-complicated appearance, we only highlight the first occurrence of the word or phrase.

Screen examples

We also make frequent use of 'screenshots' to illustrate the effect of a given procedure. However, it is not always possible to show every single step along the way so be sure to follow the mouse, keyboard and text instructions carefully.

Which Windows?

This manual has been written for Microsoft Windows 7 Home Premium, the current version of Windows that comes pre-installed on most new computers. This is almost certainly what you'll encounter when you first press that On button. Of course, there have been many previous versions of Windows, including 95, 98, Me, XP and Vista, and you may have one of those if you buy or inherit an older PC. However, you'll find that most of what we cover here is relevant on those older operating systems. We certainly recommend that you upgrade to Windows 7 if possible, but check that your hardware can handle it first. Microsoft has an upgrade advisor tool here: **http://bit.ly/d02lWz**.

1

PART 1 From delivery to desktop

Let's assume that you've just taken delivery of several rather large and heavy panic-inducing boxes. If you had just bought a television set or some hi-fi equipment, you could be reasonably confident of connecting a couple of cables, plugging it into the mains electricity and being able to sit back and enjoy the fruit of your labours. But this is a computer system, and you just *know* that it's going to stress you out.

Perhaps you've already called your colleagues, neighbours or the emergency services for assistance. But relax. In just a few pages' time, you'll be using your PC for the very first time. We're going to talk you through unpacking and setting up your shiny new computer system so that it works first time around ... and keeps on working.

PART ① A (very) potted guide to PCs

Be honest, now – how much do you really want to know about your computer? You don't have to grasp the workings of an internal combustion engine to drive a car or comprehend the mysteries of twisted-pair copper wiring to pick up the telephone. Most computer manuals (in our admittedly biased opinion) go into far too much detail, leaving you a good deal more knowledgeable but not necessarily better equipped to do something useful like writing a letter. So here instead is a brief look at the basics. We'll get through it as quickly as we possibly can.

Your computer system is essentially composed of two parts, hardware and software.

Hardware

First, let's consider the nuts and bolts.

The system unit Or, if you prefer, the case. System units are usually tall, thin 'tower' affairs these days but you can still buy squat, wide cases called, confusingly, 'desktop' PCs. There is no practical difference between the two aside from the design; a desktop PC is basically a tower case on its side. See illustration below.

The system unit has one, or maybe two, important buttons on the front: an on/off switch and, optionally, a reset switch. The first controls the power supply to the computer and the second is used to **restart** the computer if it ever 'hangs' i.e. if it ever freezes in the middle of an operation. If you have no reset switch, pressing and holding the on/off switch for about five seconds has the same effect.

Inside the system unit is a large printed circuit board known as the motherboard, or mainboard. This hosts the **processor** and **memory** and all the other electronic gubbins that make a computer smart. Everything that plays a part in your computer system connects to the **motherboard** in one way or another.

Monitor

Speakers

CD/DVD drive

Floppy disc drive

System unit

On/off switch

Reset switch

Keyboard

Mouse

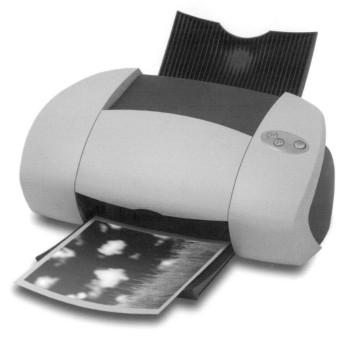

Forget the dream of a 'paperless world' – printers still have a place.

Peripherals

If the system unit is the PC proper, everything else can be called a peripheral device. But what does it all do?

Monitor A display screen on which you view images generated by your computer. Virtually all monitors now are lightweight flat-screen LCD models, whereas old monitors used a bulky, heavy *CRT* technology.

Keyboard A typewriter-like input device. Every press of a key generates a signal that the computer interprets and acts upon. Basically, it's one way of feeding instructions to your computer.

Mouse This handheld input device controls a pointer on the monitor screen. By pointing at on-screen objects and clicking the mouse's buttons, you make your computer do stuff. This is the other way of feeding instructions to your computer.

Speakers Without speakers, your computer can emit only the odd forlorn bleep. With speakers, it rocks.

Printer A device that turns computer-generated content into paper documents. Thus you might write a letter or draw a picture on your computer and print out a hard copy on your printer. Inkjet printers print in colour and are ideal for family use; laser printers generally print in black and white only but achieve a higher quality suitable for professional stationery.

Scanner A device that takes a photograph of anything you place under the lid, turns it into an electronic image and sends it to your computer. It is ideal for scanning snapshots or documents.

Drives

A drive is a device that reads *data* from and, sometimes, writes data to magnetic or optical media. In plain English, drives let you access and save information.

Hard disk drive At the heart of any PC is the hard *disk* drive. This is where files you create are saved. It is also home to the computer's operating system and application software, more of which shortly. Without a hard disk drive, your PC would be an empty shell with no memory and about as useful as a mobile phone on Mars. The hard disk drive is hidden away inside the case.

Floppy disk drive This drive used low-capacity magnetic disks. It is now completely obsolete. We include it here for nostalgic reasons alone.

CD/DVD drive A CD drive can do one or more of these: read data from a pre-recorded compact disc (CD-ROM); save data onto a blank compact disc, but just once (CD-R); and save data onto a compact disc time and time again, overwriting existing data as required (CD-RW). A CD-RW drive can do all three. A *DVD drive* can read from and write to similar discs that store a great deal more data and, of course, play movies just like the DVD player in your living room. It can also do everything that a CD drive can

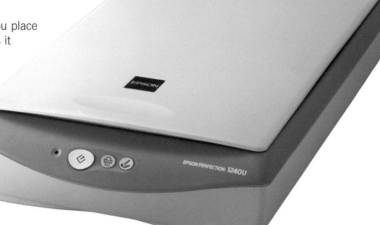

Although an optional extra, a scanner is useful for turning paper-based documents and images into computer files.

do. It is standard now to find a single drive in a new computer that combines all of the functions of CD and DVD drives. This makes life a lot simpler than it used to be!

Memory card reader This is not strictly a drive at all, but you may well find what looks like a drive with several horizontal slots built into the system unit. This is a memory card reader. You use it to *copy* files to and from memory cards used in digital cameras and music players.

Power supply

Mouse socket

Keyboard socket

Serial port

Monitor port

USB ports

Network port

Audio inputs and outputs

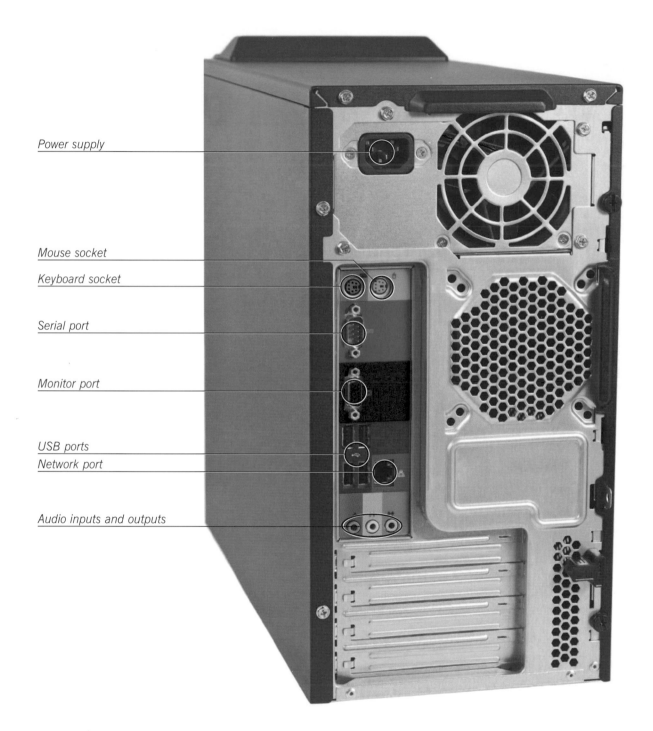

Ethernet is a standard used for connecting computers in a network.

Windows 7 Home Premium.

Interfaces

It's time to look around the back. Scary stuff? Not a bit of it. First off, near the top, you'll find a large three-pin socket for connecting the power supply. Once you've connected the power cable, you shouldn't need to bother with it again.

Just about everything else is an *interface* of some sort – that is, a port or socket used to connect other hardware devices to the system unit. In this example, we see round sockets for the mouse (green) and keyboard (purple). These are old-style sockets that you won't find on new computers. These days, mice and keyboards are connected through *USB* ports.

Next one down, coloured green, is a *serial* socket. This is now entirely obsolete but you'll still find these sockets on older hardware.

Below it, coloured blue, is the monitor socket. This is a *VGA* socket. Your computer might have a white socket instead, known as *DVI*. Or both. A white DVI socket would mean that your computer is designed for a digital monitor, whereas a blue VGA socket is designed for older analogue monitors. If you have both, you can connect two monitors to your computer and run them side by side (if you have room on your desk).

Next we see a cluster of four USB ports and next to that a network, or *Ethernet*, port. Ethernet is a standard for connecting computers to a *network*, most commonly used at home for connecting to a *router* for internet access.

Finally, we find some audio sockets for connecting speakers and plugging in a microphone or other external device.

Lower down the case, we find several slots covered with metal plates. These are slots for expansion cards. An expansion card is simply a circuit board that plugs in to the internal motherboard in order to add flexibility and expansion possibilities to your PC. This computer has no expansion cards currently installed.

Software

Software is any set of coded instructions that a computer can understand. When you press a key on the keyboard, the computer knows that something has happened; however, it takes software to turn the raw electronic signal into an instruction to display, say, the letter Q. We'll look at software in detail later but for now let's concentrate on an absolutely critical trichotomy that baffles even many experienced computer owners: the difference between the operating system, application software and driver software.

Operating system A multi-faceted software program that runs the computer. In the present case, this is a program developed by Microsoft called Windows 7 Home Premium. Windows is a graphical program, which means you interact with it by means of on-screen objects and *menus* i.e. you don't have to learn a complex language of text commands. This makes computers easy to use. It does not, however, make them entirely intuitive, which is why we've written this manual.

From now on, we will refer to the operating system simply as Windows.

Application software Although an operating system like Windows contains many useful programs that go well beyond the basics of running the computer, it is not by itself sufficient to make a PC practical in the long term. For this you need application software i.e. dedicated programs designed for specific tasks. You need application software to write a letter, *surf* the internet or play around with *digital* pictures.

From now on, we will refer to application software simply as programs.

Driver software Special code that enables a computer to interact with hardware devices. When you buy, for instance, a new scanner, you will find two types of software in the box: application software, with which to edit scanned images, but also – and more importantly – driver software. The driver tells the computer that a scanner has just been bolted on to the system, that it's this particular make and model of scanner, and that it's capable of doing X, Y and Z. Without a driver sitting between the device and the operating system, nothing happens.

From now on, we will refer to the driver software simply as drivers.

All clear? Windows runs your computer, programs let you do interesting things with it, and drivers make your hardware work.

PART 1 Preparing your workstation

Your very first task before unpacking a thing should be deciding where to put it all. Computer equipment is heavy, fragile and a pain to shift from here to there, so let's plan it properly from the outset. We'll assume here that your computer system comprises a system unit, monitor, keyboard, mouse, speakers, printer and scanner. That's pretty much the norm these days.

Workstation or desk?

Workstations come in many shapes and sizes, from corner-hugging, space-saving, vertically-stacking units to great, sprawling, semi-permanent installations. The choice is yours, but we would caution against underestimating how much room your computer needs. Even with everything tucked away, you'll still need sufficient space to site your keyboard directly in front of the monitor with a mouse mat alongside. What about the speakers? The printer and scanner? A telephone? Will you still be able to lay out documents as you work on them? Factor in a little personal elbow room, too: you will, after all, spend a good deal of time with your computer (no, really, you will).

The main attraction of a purpose-built workstation is that you can find one to fit any available space. But don't be tempted to splash out if you have a perfectly serviceable desk to hand.

Power points

Your computer system is going to require five plug sockets: one each for the system unit, monitor, speakers, printer and scanner. We would also suggest that you invest in a desk lamp, which makes it six. Invest in one or two of those power strip extensions with multiple sockets, and check that they comfortably extend to the rear of your workstation or desk. Moreover, only buy power strips with 'surge protection' built in. This will protect your valuable equipment if the electricity supply is subject to any fluctuations, such as those caused by heavy electrical equipment on the same mains circuit.

You might also consider an 'uninterruptible power supply' (i.e. a battery-powered unit that sits between your computer and the mains power and temporarily takes over in the event of a power cut).

To use the internet, you will need access to a telephone socket or a cable point. It might be worthwhile getting your telephone company to install a fresh socket behind your workstation, or perhaps installing an extension yourself. Failing that, plan how you will connect the back-end of your computer to the nearest telephone socket via a router. Trailing a cable across the carpet, under doors and up the stairs is not conducive to domestic harmony.

Also consider nearby sources of heat and light. Your computer will thank you not to be sited too close to a radiator, and you

Support your wrists with a gel-filled rest.

must allow it adequate ventilation (i.e. at least 30cm of clear space around the rear of the system unit and the monitor vents). Sit directly facing a window and you'll spend all summer squinting at the screen; sit with a window behind you and the screen will reflect the light back into your eyes. Your monitor generates its own bright images without the need for any external lighting so do your eyes a favour and avoid screen glare, even if it means compromising on the ideal site for your computer.

Are you sitting comfortably?

Ergonomics, or the study of workplace design, is more a case of common sense than hard science. When arranging your workstation, there are two main considerations: comfort and safety. By comfort, we mean that you shouldn't have to crick your neck to see the monitor, prop yourself up on cushions to use the keyboard or crawl under the desk to reach your computer's CD-ROM drive. By safety, however, we must consider the dangers of using a computer for prolonged periods. Chief amongst the hazards is Repetitive Strain Injury, or RSI, involving such unpleasant complaints as tenosynovitis, tendonitis and carpal tunnel syndrome. Regular breaks and stretching exercises are advisable during a long *session* at the desk but equally important is adopting a sensible posture. Above all, any discomfort is a sign of stress, so respect your body's signals and take action before it is too late. RSI is a debilitating and often agonising condition.

Invest in a fully-adjustable chair to save yourself from backache. A three-legged Chippendale copy liberated from the dining room really isn't up to the job.

Good posture and careful planning help avoid RSI.

Good posture begins with a straight back. A decent chair is essential but equally so is a cast-iron resolution not to hunch over your keyboard or slump in your seat.

When using the keyboard, your forearms should be horizontal and held at approximately 90° to your upper arms.

The back and the seat of your chair should both be adjustable for height and tilt. Adjustable arm rests are a good idea, and the chair should be absolutely stable. A five-legged platform is more stable than a three-legged one.

The top of your monitor screen should be no higher than eye level. Indeed, some research suggests that the monitor should ideally be positioned between 15° and 50° below eye level, much like you would hold a magazine. The screen should be at least 60cm away from your face.

Position the monitor directly in front of you, not offset to one side.

Your feet should be flat on the floor and your thighs horizontal or, preferably, tilted slightly forwards. Use a foot rest if necessary (no, not your scanner) to maintain a 90° angle between the thighs and shins. This helps support your back.

PART ① Plugging it all together

Here comes the daunting part – unpacking your new PC system and making it work. We'll assume that you've already sneaked a peep inside the boxes and panicked at the sight of endless CD-ROMs, manuals and cables. How on earth are you supposed to know where to start?

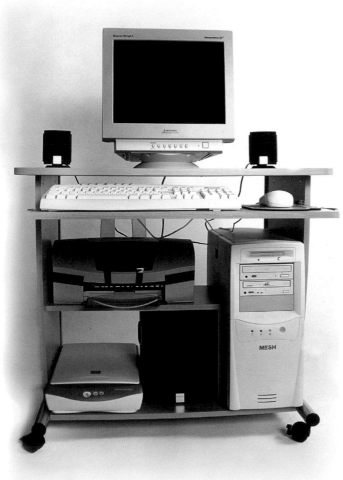

Get organised

First things first: let's unpack. Your computer system will be packed in several boxes, typically one each for the monitor, speakers, printer and scanner, and a further carton containing the system unit, keyboard, mouse and various bits and pieces. Carefully take everything out, lay it out on the floor and check it against the delivery paperwork. This may be easier said than done, of course – you may not appreciate (or particularly care) that 'ATI RADEON 8500 64MB DV (ALL IN WONDER)' refers to the computer's internal video card, so simply keep an eye open for obvious omissions. If there's no monitor, get on the blower.

Here is a list of everything delivered with our system:

- One computer in a tower system unit
- One monitor with manual
- One keyboard
- One *5.1* speaker system with cables, power supply and set-up guide
- One large, clearly illustrated and very welcome installation sheet
- One printer
- One scanner

'It'll be nice when it's finished,' you muse hopefully when confronted with boxes of unconnected hardware. And you're right . . . it will be.

Your computer may come with manuals and software discs aplenty, but we'll get you there one step at a time.

So far, so obvious. But then we came upon this little lot:

User guide The main manual! Very important.

Customer support guide Equally important. This tells you how to get *technical help*.

Two three-pin power cables One each for the system unit and the monitor.

Ethernet cable Connects the PC to a router for internet access.

Monitor adaptor This little adaptor means that we can connect an older-style CRT monitor to the modern DVI interface on the video card.

Video card manual You may need to refer to the manual to understand the *video card's* features.

Motherboard manual If you ever open up your computer to perform an upgrade, this manual will prove invaluable. Until then, keep it safe and don't give it another thought.

Windows recovery DVD This can get you out of trouble if your PC starts to experience severe problems.

Sound card CD-ROM This disc contains the drivers necessary to get the *sound card* working. However, most computer manufacturers pre-install essential software so that your computer works 'straight out of the box'. This disc would only be required if you ever had to re-install the sound card.

Video card CD-ROM Ditto.

Video-editing CD-ROM Programs for editing video footage on the PC.

CD/DVD-burning CD-ROM Programs for recording data, audio or video compilations onto blank CD and DVD discs.

Office suite CD-ROM Programs for writing letters, keeping records and doing all sorts of creative things like that. You may have been supplied with an armful of application software – or none at all.

Mouse mat A mat for the mouse.

Oh, and the mouse The mouse itself.

Phew! Little wonder people panic.

A monitor adaptor lets you connect an older-style CRT monitor (big, bulky) to a DVI video card designed for digital LCD monitors (flat, lightweight).

Laying it out

Set up the key components – system unit, monitor, keyboard and mouse – roughly as you plan to use them. Don't worry about the cables and wiring; everything can hang loose for now.

If you've acquired an older-style CRT monitor, which would only be the case if you bought your system second-hand, you will probably have to attach a swivel base to its underside first. This is usually straightforward, but start as you mean to go on and consult the monitor manual.

Now have a seat and see if it all feels just about right. Pay particular attention to any sources of glare on the monitor screen. Take the time now to make any adjustments, even if it means moving your workstation across the room or rethinking your power source. It's a good deal easier doing this now than after having made all the hardware connections.

Now bring the printer and scanner into play. Don't worry yet about any tape or security packing on these devices; simply take them from their boxes and make sure they fit their allotted space. In particular, remember that your printer will need to have input and output trays bolted on, which significantly increases its working area.

Finally, unpack and arrange your speakers. This could involve anywhere from two simple stereo speakers to four or five speakers if you opted for a 4.1 or 5.1 *'surround sound'* system. Or, indeed, no speakers at all if they are integrated within the monitor.

Unpack the smaller satellite speakers, attach any stands supplied and note the lengths of their cables. You should find that two speakers (or three in a 5.1 system) come with relatively short cables, perhaps a couple of metres each. Two others will have longer cables, typically five metres. One speaker with a short cable should be positioned either side of the monitor, equidistant from your seated position but with as much space between them as possible. The third short-cabled speaker (5.1 system only) should be sited as centrally as possible, perhaps on a shelf above the monitor or indeed perched on the monitor itself. In truth, only a true audiophile would object if you tucked it in to one side of the monitor.

The speakers with longer cables should now be located either side of and behind your seated position for the full surround sound effect.

At this point it's quite possible that all the computer salesman's patter about DVD movie soundtracks stunningly rendered in surround sound Dolby Digital will pale into insignificance when you realise that, in fact, there's just no convenient way to locate these satellites in your living room. If so, now is the time to cut your losses and settle for simple stereo sound, in which case you don't need the rear or central satellites at all.

With or without rear speakers, you will certainly want to use a **subwoofer** if one was supplied. This is a large, powerful unit that broadcasts deep bass tones. It should be located at floor level but needn't be centrally positioned (i.e. you don't have to stick it between your feet).

A 5.1 surround sound system requires careful speaker placement.

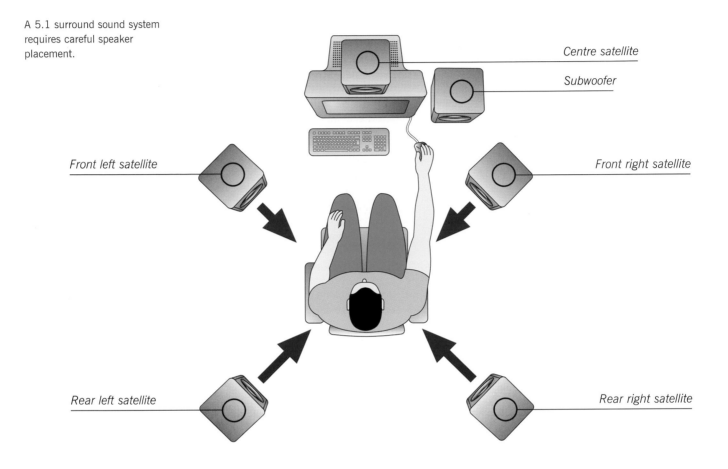

Centre satellite

Subwoofer

Front left satellite

Front right satellite

Rear left satellite

Rear right satellite

Once more, with everything roughly in place, satisfy yourself with your workstation arrangement.

Making connections

It's time to turn all this raw hardware into a working computer.

As we have already seen, the rear of the system unit hosts a range of electronic interfaces, each of which lets you connect a device to the system. Right now, you need to identify four, namely:

Monitor. This is either a blue *analogue* socket (VGA) for use with older-style CRT monitors or a white digital socket (DVI) for use with digital *LCD* monitors.

Just to confuse the issue, here we have to connect a CRT monitor to a DVI socket, hence the presence of the adaptor plug we unearthed earlier. In most cases, however, the thick white cable hard-wired to the monitor plugs straight into a VGA or DVI socket.

Keyboard. A round socket, usually colour-coded purple. The connector on the keyboard's cable is coloured correspondingly. How handy is that? Alternatively the keyboard may come with a USB connection.

Mouse. A similar story to the keyboard, but in green. Or in USB flavour.

Speakers. If you have simple stereo speakers, they will connect directly to the sound card in the system unit. However, in a surround sound system, the speakers do not connect to the sound card directly; rather, they connect to the subwoofer, which then connects to the sound card. Inevitably, all this plugging together of speakers involves a good deal of crawling around at floor level, which is why once again we exhort you to be sure that you're happy with your workstation before you make a start.

When you have identified these essentials, you can start to hook it all together.

Fancy speakers require fancy connections. Here, the five satellite speakers all plug into the subwoofer, and then the subwoofer hooks up to the system unit.

Begin with the monitor. Note how the shaped connector on the monitor cable fits the PC's socket in only one direction. Line them up and gently push the connector home, taking great care not to force it or bend the pins. Now secure the cable in position with the connector's integrated screws. Do NOT over-tighten them – the idea is merely to ensure that the connector will not slip or be easily knocked out of its socket. In this case, we are using the adaptor described on page 19.

Now connect the keyboard and mouse. Note again that the pins on the connector and the holes in the socket must be carefully aligned. Follow the colour coding or look for descriptive stickers on the case next to the sockets – or, if you've a USB keyboard and/or mouse, simply plug them into any USB ports. Place the keyboard directly in front of the monitor on your desktop and the mouse on its mat to either the right or the left depending upon whether you're right- or left-handed.

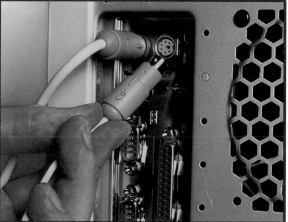

The precise method for wiring up the speaker system depends upon your equipment but you will have been supplied with a guide. In this case, we have five satellite speakers to connect to the subwoofer. The subwoofer then connects to the sound card by means of three 3.5mm audio jacks. Take the time to ensure that each speaker is connected to the correct channel on the subwoofer (e.g. the speaker that sits to the left of the monitor on your workstation should be connected to the channel marked 'front left').

Connect the three-pin power cables to the system unit and monitor and plug them into the power strip. If the PC's power supply unit has a voltage selector, take a second to check that it is set correctly for your country (e.g. 240V in the UK). The PC's power supply unit may also have an on/off switch; if so, flick it to the on position now. Also plug the subwoofer into the power strip. Look for a power switch or button on the subwoofer case and turn it on. Volume controls should be set about a third of the way between minimum and maximum.

And that's that. Just to refresh:

- The monitor should be connected to the system unit's video card.
- The keyboard and mouse should be connected to the system unit.
- The satellite speakers should be connected to the subwoofer.
- The subwoofer should be connected to the system unit's sound card.
- The system unit, monitor and subwoofer should all be plugged into a surge-protected power strip.

Now plug the power strip into the mains electricity and flick the switch. Ready for some action? Turn to the next section.

PART ① Turning on for the first time ... and off again

Caller: 'Hello, technical support? I need help! My computer won't work properly.'

Technical Support: 'Hmm. Have you tried booting it?'

Caller: 'Hold on ...'

A sickening crunch is heard.

Caller: 'No, that didn't seem to help.'

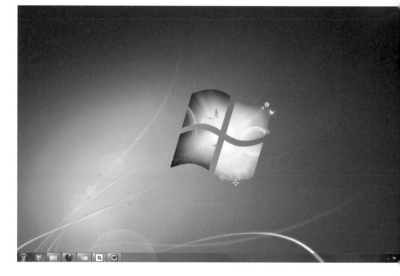

Your first encounter with Windows Desktop and that all-important Start button.

Boot camp

To 'boot' (or 'power-up') a computer is to switch it on, so let's do just that. Shuffle your computer system back into the right arrangement on your workstation – everything may have moved about when you made the connections – and take a seat at your workstation.

It's good practice to turn on the monitor first because it means you can read any messages that appear on screen. Do this now. There's usually a biggish button on the front, but check the manual if you're not certain.

Now push the larger button on the front of the system unit. Hear that whirring sound? That's the internal cooling fans springing into action, without which your computer would melt. Watch the screen and you'll likely see some gobbledegook in white letters on a black background. That's fine; ignore it. Soon, you will see a Windows welcome screen followed quickly by the Windows Desktop. You will even hear a congratulatory tune tinkle forth from your speakers. This is Windows saying hello.

Exactly what you see at this point depends upon how your computer manufacturer has set up your system but so long as there's a round button with the Windows flag in the very bottom left corner of the screen – hereafter referred to as the Start *button* – you've made it. This is the Desktop. Windows 7 is up and running and ready for action.

The great escape

Here's an oddity: the very first thing you should do having turned on your computer is turn it straight back off again. This is because it is very, very important to learn the correct approach and follow it every time. Here's another oddity: switching off begins with the Start button.

We're going to practise using the mouse shortly, so for now you may not find the following steps natural or easy. But just take your time and you'll get there (well, hopefully – now might be a good time to forget all about that client mentioned in the introduction).

? QUICK Q & A

How do I change my Desktop picture to something more interesting?

🖱 Anywhere on the Desktop

🖱 Personalize

🖱 Any of the themes that you see in the Personalization window

🖱 The cross at the very top right of the window to close the window

Windows 7 comes with a range of themes that change the overall look and colour scheme of your computer. You can personalise just about any element, including the transparency of windows and background images. We're using the plain Windows 7 theme in these screenshots.

? QUICK Q & A

Why does my monitor/ hard disk keep turning itself off after a couple of hours?

This is all to do with power-saving settings. Computers are designed to run all day and night but you can save on electricity bills by having them click into standby mode at times of inactivity. The settings can be accessed and changed here:

🖱 Start

⌨ Power Options (in the Search panel just above the Start button)

🖱 Power Options

① Start

When you move the mouse around on its mat, the onscreen pointer matches its movements. Push the mouse forwards (i.e. towards the far side of your desk) and the pointer moves up the screen; slide it to the right and the pointer follows suit. Your task is to make the pointer point at the Start **button** in the lower left corner of the screen. When it's in position, press and release the left mouse button with your index finger. This is called clicking. If the mouse jerks out of position at this point, just use your other hand to keep it steady and persevere. Don't worry, this will all become second nature soon enough!

② Shut down

When you make a successful 'click', a menu pops up, above the Start button. At the bottom right of this menu, you'll see an option to Shut down. Move the mouse until the pointer points straight at this button and click it.

Clicking the arrow to the right of Shut down gives you some further options, which we go on to explore.

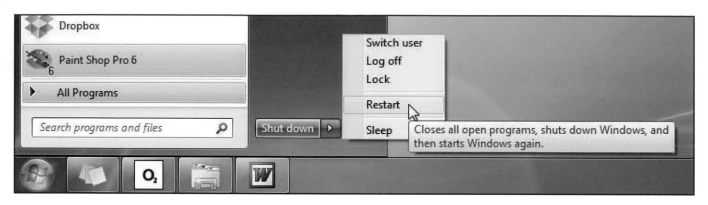

Restart

Sometimes, you may want your computer to turn itself back on again immediately. For instance, some software programs require you to restart your computer after installation.

  Start

  Click the arrow to the right of Shut down

  Restart

Your computer will turn off and straight back on again.

Sleep

If you're planning to leave your computer for a while but know you'll be returning, you can save power by putting it to 'sleep'. In sleep mode, your computer remembers what it was doing and will resume exactly where you left it. However, the monitor will turn off and the screen will go blank. To resume full operation, simply click the mouse or press any key on the keyboard.

  Start

  Click the arrow to the right of Shut down

  Sleep

![Windows Start menu screenshot showing Dropbox, Paint Shop Pro 6, All Programs, Search programs and files box, and the Shut down menu expanded with Switch user, Log off, Lock, Restart, Sleep options. A tooltip reads "Switch users without closing programs."]

Switch user

As we'll see in Appendix 2, your computer can be set up to run multiple 'user accounts'. This allows you to, for instance, have your computer set up in different ways for Mum, Dad and the kids. Each account can be personally configured and customised, so Mum might see only her e-mail, Dad might see only his and the kids have a different background image and shortcuts to favourite games. To switch between accounts, here's what to do.

 Start

 Click the arrow to the right of Shut down

Switch user

Note that you only have a choice here if you have already set up more than one user account (see Appendix 2). Click on one of the other user accounts to open it. The user account that you were in previously will continue running in the background, completely hidden, so you can easily repeat this move to return to that account.

Reboot

In thankfully rare circumstances, your computer may freeze or 'hang' completely. This means that nothing happens when you use the keyboard or click the mouse and everything is completely unresponsive. It's as if your computer has died on you, although the monitor will still be working. In this situation, the easiest option is to force your computer to restart. However, because you can't use the mouse to click the Start button, you have to use the power button on the computer's case. Press and hold it for about five seconds until the power goes off, then release it. Wait about ten seconds and press it again to turn your computer back on. If you see a black screen with white text asking if you want to start Windows normally, select this option.

PART 2 First steps

OK, so you've set up your computer and turned it on and off. Our guess is that you're itching to do something *useful* with it … but we're going to crave your indulgence and ask you to hang fire a while longer. These next few pages are absolutely critical: if you can master mouse and keyboard control right from the outset, even at the most basic level, all that follows will be so much easier.

We'll also get your printer and scanner up and running in this section.

PART ② Make friends with your mouse

A natural extension of your hand, or a slippery lump of plastic that slides around out of control and drives you to distraction? Like it or loathe it, the mouse is such an integral part of modern computing that nothing pays dividends like mastering it early.

Anatomy of a mouse

Windows is a graphical operating system for your computer, which means that you get to work with pictures and other visual clues instead of having to type text commands (as in the *bad old days*). The mouse enables you to interact with these graphics.

As in Part 1, you can see this by moving the mouse on its mat while Windows is running – every motion is replicated by the onscreen pointer.

Hardware-wise, the average modern mouse has two buttons with a wheel lodged between them. The left button is the primary button – i.e. it is used most frequently and performs most common tasks – while the right button generally invokes special shortcuts. The wheel, if present, can have a number of functions but is mainly used to 'scroll' through long documents and *web pages*.

Some mice have an integrated rubber ball on their undersides and work best on hard rubber mouse mats that help the ball rotate freely and accurately. Others, called optical mice, use a light instead of a ball and work on just about any surface. With an optical mouse, you don't need a mouse mat as it should work just fine directly on your desk or workstation. The exception is if you have a glass-covered surface, on which a mouse mat is a must.

Hold your mouse gently but firmly as shown below with your index and middle fingers resting lightly on the buttons. Practise just sliding it around the mat for a while and watch the onscreen pointer mimic its movements. It's very relaxing. Unfortunately, it doesn't get you very far.

The mouse pointer is an onscreen arrow controlled by your mouse. Use it to, er, point at things and click them.

There's no need to squeeze the life out of your mouse – hold it gently, get your fingers in position and practise until it feels natural.

Keep your mouse free from fluff to keep it running smoothly.

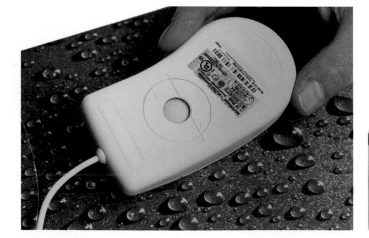

Some funky things to do with a mouse

Here, then, are the key mouse concepts used in everyday home computing. Refer to the conventions on page 8 for a refresher on the symbols used below.

Point-and-click. *This is where you make the onscreen pointer point at something, like an icon or a menu, and then press and release the left mouse button. It makes a satisfying clicking sound, hence the term 'click'. This is generally abbreviated to, for example, 'click the Start button'.*

 Start

Start

Use the mouse to make the onscreen pointer point at the Start button in the bottom-left corner of your screen and click the left button once. This makes the Start Menu pop up. Now click the button again to make the menu disappear. What could be simpler?

Double click. *Instead of pressing and releasing the mouse button once, here you click it twice in rapid succession. Why? Well, in certain circumstances, the first click merely 'selects' the given object and the second click 'activates' it. Unless we specifically say 'double click', assume that any instruction refers to a single click.*

Recycle Bin on the Desktop

To open a file or launch a program, you need to click it twice quickly. Your Desktop will almost certainly have a few icons, or pictures, on it. Double click any icon to open the associated program or file. We've chosen the Recycle Bin here.

Don't fret if you struggle with this one, particularly if the mouse moves slightly between clicks or you don't manage to click quickly enough to launch the program or file. We'll show you a way to make life easier in a moment.

③

Drag. *Another absolutely central mouse operation. Dragging involves a click-and-hold manoeuvre whereby you point at something, press the left mouse button and then keep the button depressed instead of releasing it straight away.*

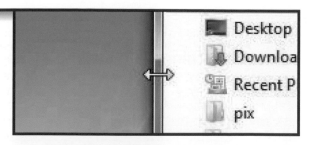

 Recycle Bin icon

Double click the Recycle Bin icon on the Desktop to open a window. Move the onscreen pointer right to one edge of the window. See how it suddenly changes shape to a double-headed arrow? Your task now is to click and hold the left mouse button just as the pointer changes. Then, keeping the left mouse button depressed, move the double-headed arrow slightly to the left and slightly to the right. The window will expand and contract accordingly. When you release the mouse button, the window stays the way you leave it.

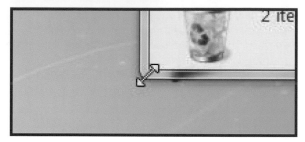

Now try the same technique with the top and bottom edge of the window and expand or contract it vertically.

Finally – and this is much trickier – point at one of the window's corners and watch the pointer change shape to a slanted double-headed arrow. Now click, hold and drag in a diagonal direction. This resizes the window horizontally and vertically simultaneously.

When you're finished, click the small cross in the top-right corner to close the Recycle Bin window.

④

Drag-and-drop. *A closely related discipline that involves moving an object rather than resizing it. The initial technique is just the same.*

 Recycle Bin icon

This time, point at the middle of the Title Bar i.e. the wide, coloured upper-edge of the window that tells you the name of the window – in this case, Recycle Bin. The pointer will not change shape. Now click the left mouse button and, keeping the button depressed as before, drag the entire window up, down and all around the Desktop. See how it follows the movements of the mouse? At any time, you can release the mouse button to 'drop' the window in a new position. Again, close the window when you're through by clicking the small cross in the top-right corner.

Well, we're getting a little ahead of ourselves here, playing around with serious concepts like icons and windows before offering any real explanation as to what these things are and how they work. It's all a bit chicken and egg, really – it's important to be competent with the mouse and keyboard before tackling Windows but acquiring this competency inevitably involves using Windows. Still, not to worry. It is all good practice and will all make perfect sense soon enough.

Right-clicking

All computer mice have (at least) two buttons. Most of the time, you'll use the left button but we'd like to encourage you to experiment with the right button as well. Wherever you are – in Windows, using a program, browsing the web, writing an email – just take a second to click the right button and see what happens. Don't worry, you can't possibly do any harm: the right button invariably opens a menu with some options. What's important is that this menu is context-sensitive. That is, the menu options change according to where you are and what you're doing at the time. Here are some examples.

 1

Recycle Bin icon

Properties

*The Recycle Bin is a holding area for files and folders that you **delete** before they are permanently destroyed. In the Properties **dialogue box**, you can determine how much of your hard disk space is reserved for this purpose. Don't change anything; the point is simply that you can manage this setting with a simple right click.*

2

Computer icon

Properties

This manoeuvre opens up a world of possibilities connected with managing your computer's settings. You can get to these settings the long way around by clicking Start > Control Panel and finding your way through the maze – or you can use this shortcut.

Right clicking any icon on your computer generally launches a menu relating to that program or file.

3

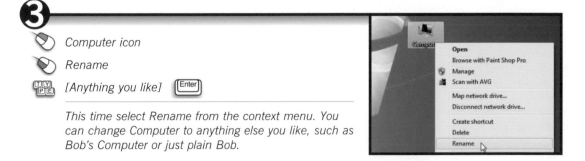

Computer icon

Rename

[Anything you like] [Enter]

This time select Rename from the context menu. You can change Computer to anything else you like, such as Bob's Computer or just plain Bob.

4

🖱️ *Clock*

Let's say your computer is showing the wrong time. How do you adjust the clock? Well, you could spend an age trying to figure this out but instead try right clicking it. Up pops a menu that includes this option: Adjust Date/Time. Again, a right click gives you access to the most likely tools you need at the time.

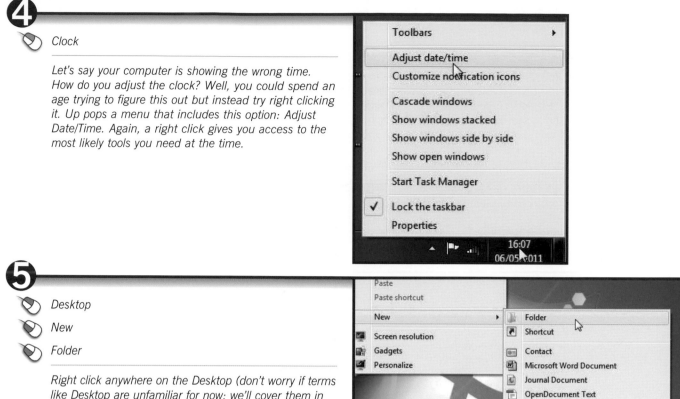

5

🖱️ *Desktop*

🖱️ *New*

🖱️ *Folder*

Right click anywhere on the Desktop (don't worry if terms like Desktop are unfamiliar for now; we'll cover them in detail in Part 3). Now create a new folder using these simple steps. It will be called New Folder, which is less than useful. So now repeat Step 3 and call it something meaningful like My Notes. You can create folders anywhere in Windows using this right-click route.

6

🖱️ *New Folder icon*

🖱️ *Delete*

🖱️ *Yes*

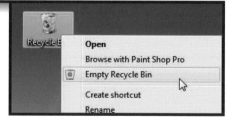

Let's say you don't really want a new folder on your Desktop after all, or that you want to do away with any other folder or file. There are various ways to achieve this but the quickest is by right clicking it and selecting Delete. Windows will ask you to confirm your intentions. The folder will then be moved to the Recycle Bin.

7

🖱️ *Recycle Bin icon*

🖱️ *Empty Recycle Bin*

As we mentioned in Step 1, the Recycle Bin stores files and folders when you delete them, just in case you later want to get one back again. If you want to completely remove the Recycle Bin's entire contents, all you need is … yes, a right click.

Incidentally, you can permanently delete any file or folder without going through the Recycle Bin holding stage. To do this, select the item you want to delete and hold down the Shift key while performing Step 6. That item will then be gone forever. Take care with this, as there's no way back.

Practice makes perfect

So much for the theory. But having already used the mouse to shut down your computer, you may be worried that you'll never get the hang of the thing. Here's an easy and fun way to practise. First, turn on your computer. Then do this:

 Start

 Solitaire [in the search panel]

 Solitaire

What we have here is Windows' own electronic version of the card game Solitaire, or Patience, and it's a great way to develop accurate mouse control. These directions obviously relate to one particular deal of the cards but just apply the general principles.

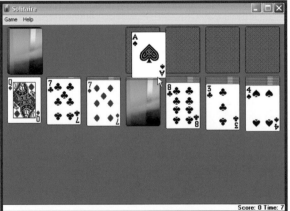

The Ace of any suit can be dragged to one of the vacant stacking areas above the main playing area. Here the Ace of Spades happens to be in column four. Point at the card, click and hold the left mouse button, then carefully drag the card to the leftmost stacking area. Now release the mouse button. Don't worry if you mess it up a few times, as the card will simply snap back to its original position on the 'table'.

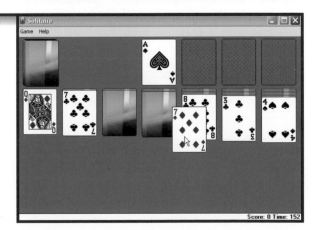

To move the red Seven onto the black Eight (or whatever), click on the card and drag and drop it into position i.e. release the mouse button when it's positioned roughly over the Eight of Clubs. You don't have to be too precise. See how it automatically snaps into place? Move as many cards as you can at this point.

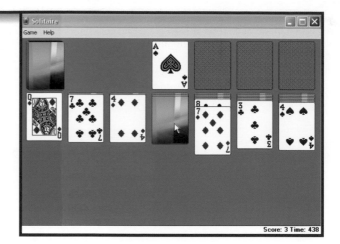

Now you need to flip over any newly-exposed cards. Point at each in turn and click once to turn it over. If this opens up new playing possibilities, drag and drop the cards as before. The Two of any suit may be dragged away from the main playing area and stacked on top of the relevant Ace in a stacking area, followed by the Three and the Four and so forth.

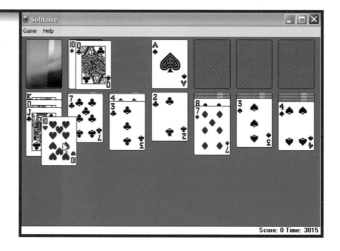

To deal some new cards three at a time, click the deck in the top-left corner. Drag and drop any suitable cards into the main playing area: in this case, the Ten of Hearts can go to the Jack of Clubs.

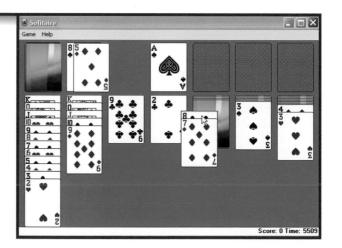

You can also drag a stack of cards from one column to another: in this case, the Eight of Clubs and the Seven of Diamonds from column five onto the Nine of Diamonds in column two. It's a little fiddly but the trick is to click onto the exposed upper-edge of the black Eight. The Seven remains locked to the Eight as you drag-and-drop the cards onto the red Nine.

7 When the deck has been fully dealt, a circle appears in the now-empty dealing area. Click the circle once to make the remaining deck jump back to the dealing area, and click again to start the dealing afresh. Keep moving cards to the Ace stacks whenever possible and see if you can clear the entire playing area.

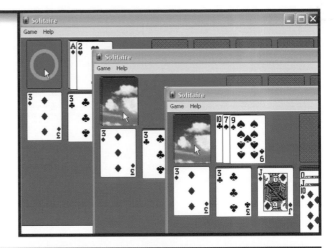

8

Game

Deal

At any time, you can begin a fresh game by clicking the Game button on the Toolbar above the playing area. When the dropdown menu appears, click Deal.

9

Help

View Help

We've rather taken it for granted that you know how to play Solitaire! If not, consult the Help menu. This is a good practice that will stand you in good stead when you come to work with more advanced application software later.

You might care to experiment with your mouse wheel at this point (if your mouse has a wheel). Roll it backwards and forwards to make the Help page scroll up and down. You can also click any of the blue links, such as 'To start a game', to see more information.

When you're finished, click the small, square cross button located at the very top-right corner of the Help window. This closes the window and returns you to the game.

To close the Solitaire program itself, click the cross in the top-right corner of the window. There, it's as simple as that. Once you can comfortably drag-and-drop single or stacked cards from one column to another, deal from the deck and start a new game, you can truly say that you have mastered mouse control. What's more, you have learned a good deal about Windows (and windows) in the process without even trying!

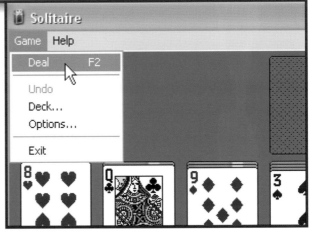

Restraining the rodent

If, however, you really struggle with these practice exercises, there is a way to make the mouse more malleable. Proceed as follows:

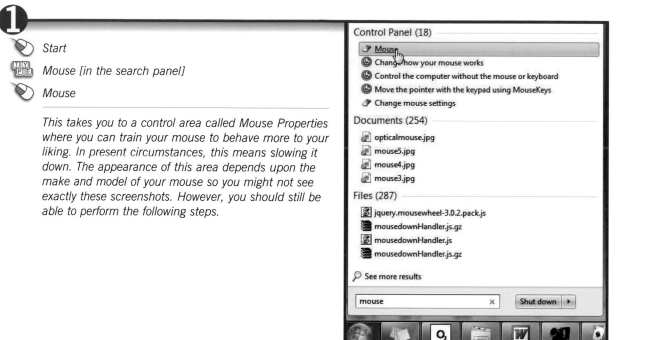

Start

Mouse [in the search panel]

Mouse

This takes you to a control area called Mouse Properties where you can train your mouse to behave more to your liking. In present circumstances, this means slowing it down. The appearance of this area depends upon the make and model of your mouse so you might not see exactly these screenshots. However, you should still be able to perform the following steps.

Pointer Options

Open the Pointer Options tab. A tab works like a divider in a folder, separating the contents into similar subject matter. To open a tab and view its contents, simply point at the title and click once.

3

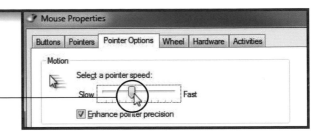

 [move slider]

 Apply

In the Motion area, you will see a graphical representation of a sliding scale. This relates to the sensitivity of the onscreen pointer in relation to your mouse (i.e. the closer the slider is to the Fast end of the spectrum, the faster the pointer travels across the screen). Click the slider control, drag it towards the left end of the scale, and release the mouse button just before it reaches Slow. Now slide the mouse around on its mat and note how you have to make big movements to move the pointer a small distance. If you like the effect, click the Apply button. If not, keep experimenting with the slider until you find a pointer speed that feels comfortable. Do not click the OK button until you have completed Step 4.

4

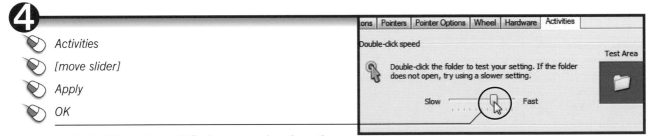

 Activities

 [move slider]

 Apply

 OK

In the Activities tab, you'll find a way to slow down the mouse's double-click speed. This is ideal if you have trouble double clicking quickly enough. Drag the slider to the Slow end of the scale. You should now be able to test your new setting by double clicking a folder. Experiment until you can open and close the folder with a double click every time, even if it means using the very slowest setting. Finally, click the Apply button to confirm the change and then click OK to close the Mouse Properties window.

FIRST STEPS

PART 2 Get to grips with your keyboard

Having looked in some detail at the mouse, we now turn to the keyboard. Although it's actually possible to operate a computer entirely with the keyboard – that is, the keyboard can do anything the mouse can do, and more besides – in practice you'll use the mouse and keyboard in tandem. Certainly, until speech recognition technology comes of age (current forecast: 12 June 2179), you'll use it every time you need to write a letter or type a command.

Anatomy of a keyboard

Like the mouse, a keyboard is an input device (i.e. it lets you interact with your computer). On pages 42–43, we see a standard-issue-type keyboard with 102 keys (plus three special Windows-specific keys).

To use it, you press the keys lightly, either one at a time or occasionally in combinations of two or three. If a combination is called for – let's say [Ctrl] + [S] – this means that you press *and hold* the [Ctrl] key and then press the [S] key with [Ctrl] still depressed.

A good combination to practise – if only because it's as hard as it gets – is [Ctrl] + [Alt] + [Del]. You can achieve this in several ways but you'll certainly need both hands. Our favoured approach is pressing and holding [Ctrl] with the ring finger on the left hand, then pressing and holding [Alt] with the index finger on the same hand, and finally pressing [Del] with any finger at all on the right hand. This three-key combination summons the useful Windows Task Manager (see page 92). For now, however, simply press the [Esc] key to make it go away.

You may or may not wish to learn to touch-type. If so, there are plenty of software programs around that can help; or, of course, you could seek out a tutor. With instruction, you will learn how to position your hands correctly and which finger to use for each key. But quite frankly we couldn't give a hoot about any of that right now. Feel free to use your keyboard in any manner you choose, even if it means stabbing each key with a solitary digit or poking them with a pencil.

Guide to the main sections of a computer keyboard

Alphanumeric keys. These are the familiar typewriter keys laid out in the standard QWERTY arrangement (this refers to the first six keys on the top line). Here we find all the letters of the alphabet, numbers 0–9 and the essential punctuation symbols.

Within and around this block, there are several important keys that take some further explaining.

Esc. *The get-me-out-of-here-sharpish key. As a rule, the* Esc *key cancels the current operation or closes a dialogue box. Press one of the* Windows *keys to make the Start Menu pop up and* Esc *to make it disappear again (yes, you've already done this back on page 31 but isn't it fun?).*

Tab. *Just like on a typewriter, this indents paragraphs several spaces to the right.*

Caps Lock. *Press this key once and every letter key you type is printed in upper case; press it again to restore the keys to lower case. IF YOU LEAVE IT TURNED ON, YOUR TYPING WILL LOOK LIKE THIS.* Caps lock *is an example of a 'toggle' key – one press for on, another press for off.*

Shift. *You can also turn on upper case by pressing and holding this key as you type. Typically, you would capitalise the first letter of the first word in a sentence with the* Shift *key as it's quicker than turning the* Caps lock *function on and off again. The* Shift *key also lets you access the uppermost symbol on any key that has two possibilities. The number* 1 *key, for instance, prints an exclamation mark when you hold down* Shift. *Note that there are two* Shift *keys on your keyboard. They are entirely interchangeable.*

Function keys. *Labelled* F1 *through to* F12, *these keys conjure up certain functions in certain programs. We won't be bothering with them but there's one useful shortcut you should know: in Windows, the* F1 *key acts as a shortcut to the Help & Support Centre.*

Spacebar. *This simply adds a space between words as you type.*

Ctrl. *Like the* Shift *key, this does nothing on its own but rather must be used in combination with other keys. For instance, pressing* Ctrl *and the letter* S *key together is a quick way of saving a document in most programs. There are two* Ctrl *keys.*

Windows. *Pressing the special* Windows *key, which is denoted by a flag, has the same effect as clicking the Start button. It also works as a combination key but we won't be calling upon its services. There are two* Windows *keys.*

Alt. *Yet another combination key that must be used in conjunction with other keys to have any effect. The second* Alt *key is actually called* Alt Gr. *We have absolutely no idea what it does and have never used it, so let's just give it a miss.*

Shift. *(see details bottom left)*

Backspace. *This key moves the cursor to the left one space at a time, and **deletes** any previous character. See the practical exercise with WordPad on page 45 for examples.*

Delete. *A key with many functions but in word processing it is generally used to erase the character immediately to the right of the current typing point. We'll see how it works in a moment.*

Shortcut keys. *Many keyboards now feature an extra array of buttons that offer useful shortcuts e.g. launch an email program or web browser, navigate backwards and forwards through web pages, and adjust the speaker volume – all without touching the mouse. Nice to have but strictly non-essential.*

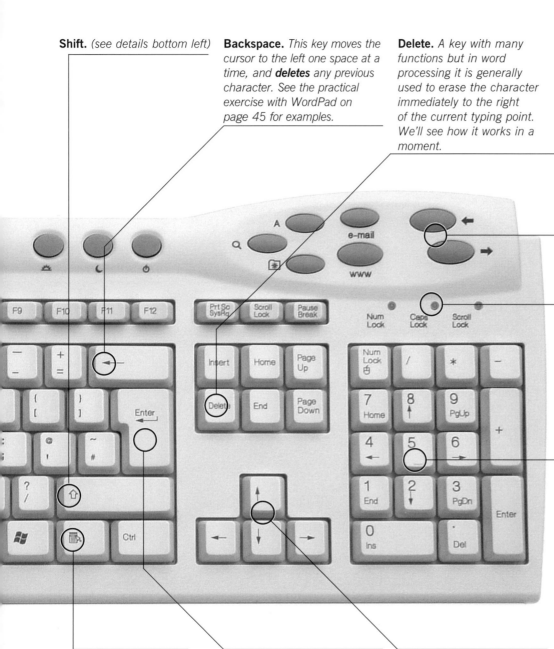

Lights. *Your keyboard also has three little status lights. One illuminates whenever the* Num lock *feature is active and another whenever* Caps lock *is on. The third relates to* Scroll lock*, a mysterious key that we have no knowledge of nor interest in.*

Numeric keypad. *With the keyboard's Num Lock function active (the **default** option when your computer starts; otherwise press* Num lock *) these calculator-style keys duplicate the number keys in the top row of the main section of the keyboard.*

With the Num Lock function disabled, the 2*,* 4*,* 6 *and* 8 *keys work just like a second set of arrow keys. The Home key takes you straight to the start of a line or the beginning of a web page; the End key takes you to the end. The Page Up/Page Down keys let you quickly scroll through an open document or web page one page, or screen, at a time.*

Shortcut. *This key has the same effect as clicking the right mouse button (see the explanation of right-clicking on page 33).*

Enter. *This works primarily like the carriage return key on a traditional typewriter (i.e. starts a new line). There's a second* Enter *key tucked away at the very bottom-right corner of your keyboard. Also known as the Return key.*

Arrow keys. *This block of four arrows is primarily used to move the blinking cursor around the text on a printed page. What's a blinking cursor? Wait for page 44.*

Practice makes perfect once again

OK, it's time to get a-clicking and put all this theory into practice. Again, we're going to jump the gun slightly and have you working with a Windows program, but just follow the directions closely and you'll have no difficulty. First, turn on your computer.

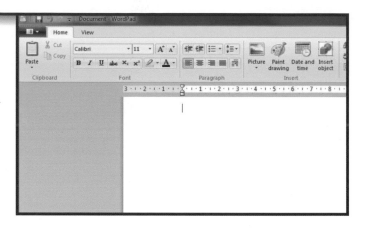

 Start

WordPad [in the search panel]

 WordPad

What we have here is the basic but functional word processor program that comes with Windows. You wouldn't write War and Peace *with WordPad but it can certainly help you master your keyboard with some simple exercises.*

First, click anywhere in the big white space. This, incidentally, is your computer's graphical representation of a sheet of paper. See that small vertical line blinking away in the top-left corner? This is technically known as the 'insertion point' because it's the point at which new text will be inserted, but we'll just call it the blinking cursor. Note that you still have a mouse pointer: just move the mouse around a bit and you'll see the familiar arrow dart around the screen. Confusing, isn't it? However, it's really important to recognise from the outset that these are quite distinct. The mouse pointer does what it always does – lets you control your computer – but the blinking cursor is contained within the page.

Press and hold down shift, press the letter T key, then release shift. There, you've just made a capital T. Now type H, I and S, and press the spacebar once. In our shorthand, this is:

What you have here is a fully fledged word. Now continue as follows (just take it slow and steady):

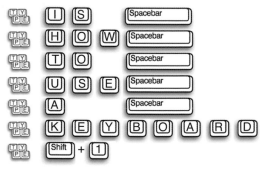

If all went well, you should now be looking at this sentence in WordPad: 'This is how to use a keyboard!' Press [Enter] *once, and note how the blinking cursor moves down to a fresh line. Press* [Enter] *again and it moves down the page still further. Now press* [Backspace] *twice to return the blinking cursor to the end of your sentence.*

Experiment with the group of arrow keys. Each press of the [←] *key moves the blinking cursor one character to the left. Keep pressing it until you reach the beginning of the first word. Now use the* [→] *to move the blinking cursor back through the text. This time, however, pause when the blinking cursor is just to the right of the letter 'o' in the word 'to'. Press the* [Backspace] *key twice to delete the word.*

 [Shift] + [I].

Your sentence has changed to: 'This is how I use a keyboard!' That very simple edit shows the power of word processing.

This time, we want to change the word 'a' to 'my' but let's proceed slightly differently. Use the arrow keys to position the blinking cursor just to the left of the word 'a', then press [Del]. *The effect is the same – you're deleting a word – but this time you've rubbed out characters to the right of the blinking cursor rather than to the left. Now press* [M] *followed by* [Y].
Your sentence should now read: 'This is how I use my keyboard!' Keep practising with the arrow keys until you're comfortable positioning the blinking cursor anywhere within your sentence.

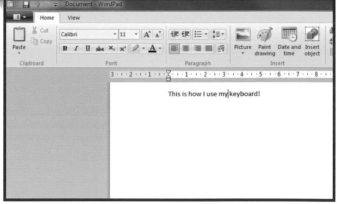

Move the blinking cursor to the right of the exclamation point and press [Enter] *twice. Now type:*

You should now have three rows of three numbers. Use the arrow keys to move the blinking cursor to the left of number 4.

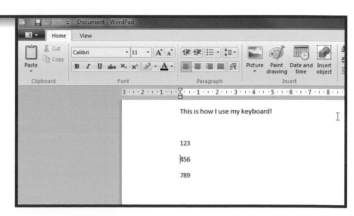

7

Now press the `Tab` key. This block of numbers will now be indented on the page. Move down to the beginning of the next block (i.e. to the left of number 7) and press `Tab` twice. This block will now be indented further. To remove the indents, position the blinking cursor just to the left of the numbers and use the `Backspace` key. Alternatively, position the blinking cursor at the very beginning of the line and use the `Del` key. This is simple formatting but already you can see how easy it is to arrange your words and numbers on a sheet of paper.

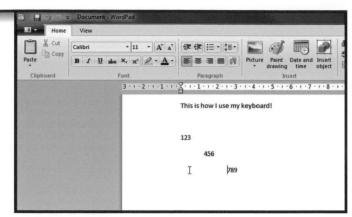

8

Finally, for now, return to your original sentence. Use the arrow keys to position the blinking cursor between the 'd' of 'keyboard' and the exclamation point. Now type:

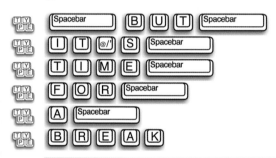

Your new text is inserted straight into the original sentence, and everything to the right of the blinking cursor – in this case, just the exclamation point – shuffles along to make space. You can't do that on a typewriter!

(Note that `@/'` is one of those dual function keys where a simultaneous press of the `Shift` key would have printed the @ character instead of an apostrophe.)
Now go and make a cup of tea, but leave everything just as it is.

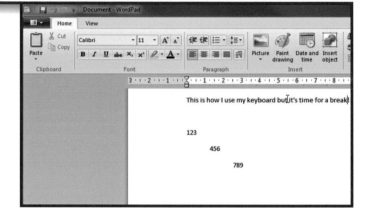

9

Ready for something a little fancier? You may have noticed that the mouse pointer changes shape depending on where in the window it happens to be. If you point at any of the buttons or menu options – File, Edit, View and so on – it looks like a normal pointer. However, if you move the pointer into the white page area, it changes to an 'I' shape. This is called an 'I-beam', and it offers an alternative way to manipulate text on the page.

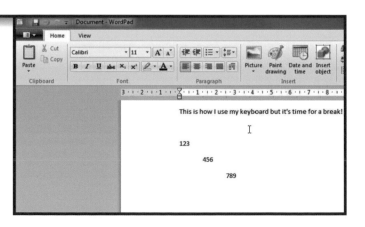

10 Using the mouse, position the I-beam between the 'k' of 'break' and the exclamation point, and click once. The blinking cursor now moves to this position on the page. Don't worry if you miss a few times – just keep trying. If at any time the text becomes accidentally 'highlighted' (see Step 12 below), click on a blank spot on the page away from the text and the highlighting will disappear. Some people find the I-beam an easier way to position the blinking cursor within text than the arrow keys; others prefer the keyboard. Either way, you now have a choice.

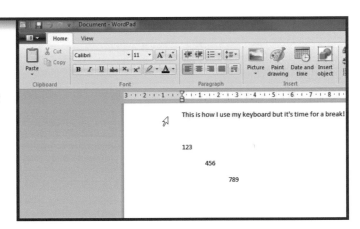

11 Now move the mouse pointer to the beginning of your sentence and watch how it changes. As it approaches the first letter of the first word, it maintains an I-beam shape – but when you position it just to the left of the first word, it takes on the shape of an arrow. In contrast to the standard mouse pointer arrow, however, this arrow points to the right rather than to the left. What you have here is a 'selection tool'.

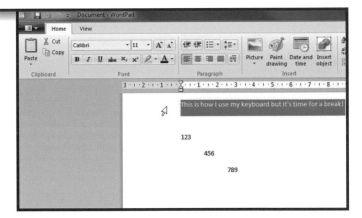

12 To see it in action, click once just as the mouse pointer turns from an I-beam into the selection tool. As if by magic, the entire line of text that it's pointing at becomes highlighted. This means that you can treat that text as a single unit and 'process' it in any way you choose. You might drag the sentence from one part of the page to another, for example, or change the font size or colour.

13 But for now, let's just delete our text. With the text highlighted, press the key. Now highlight any remaining text or numbers line-by-line with the selection tool and delete the lot until you have a blank page. Finally, close WordPad by clicking the cross in the top-right corner of the window. The program will ask you if you want to save changes to the document. Click the Don't Save button.

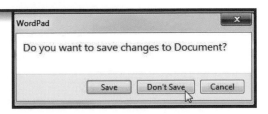

Sedating the keyboard

The thing that most people find trickiest about the keyboard is pressing and releasing the keys quickly enough. If you hold down a key for fractionally too long, the character is repeated on the pageeee (oops, there's an extra e or three right there). Having tried the exercises above, you'll know whether this applies to you. If so, here's how to make life a little easier. Proceed as follows:

1

Start

Keyboard [in the search panel]

Keyboard

This takes you to a control area called Keyboard Properties. The appearance of this area depends upon the make and model of your keyboard so you might not see exactly these screenshots. However, you should still be able to perform the following steps.

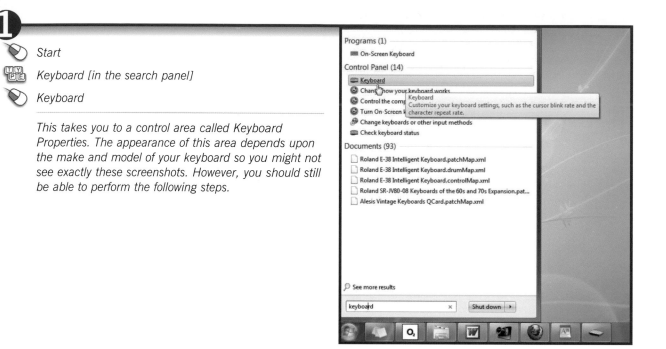

2

Speed

Open the Speed tab, or look in each tab until you find a section called Character Repeat. As a reminder, a tab is like a divider in a folder, separating the contents into related groups. To select a tab, simply point at the title – in this case Speed, – and click once.

3 [test repeat rate]

Within the Character Repeat section, you will find a testing area that looks like a white rectangle. Point at this with mouse pointer and click once. A blinking cursor will appear within the box. This is your cue to start typing. Type any word or phrase and note how quickly a character repeats when you don't release the key quickly enough. If you run out of space, use the Backspace key to delete your text.

Keyboard Properties

Speed | Hardware

Character repeat

Repeat delay:
Long —————————————— Short

Repeat rate:
Slow —————————————— Fast

Click here and hold down a key to test repeat rate:

testinggggggggggggg

Cursor blink rate

None —————————————— Fast

OK | Cancel | Apply

4 [move Repeat Delay slider]

[move Repeat Rate slider]

Apply

OK

If you find that your natural typing speed is too slow and extraneous letters keep appearing, you have two options. Repeat Delay governs how quickly a second character is printed after a key is pressed. The longer the delay, the less the chance of unwanted repeat characters. Repeat Rate determines how quickly subsequent characters then appear. The slower the rate, the fewer unwanted repeat characters. So, click-and-hold the slider controls in turn and move Repeat Delay to the Long end of the spectrum and Repeat Rate to Slow. Click anywhere in the test box again and you should find that your keyboard is now much more forgiving.
Click the Apply button to confirm the changes, and then click OK to close the Keyboard Properties window.

Keyboard Properties

Speed | Hardware

Character repeat

Repeat delay:
Long —————————————— Short

Repeat rate:
Slow —————————————— Fast

Click here and hold down a key to test repeat rate:

testinggggggggggggg

Cursor blink rate

None —————————————— Fast

OK | Cancel | Apply

PART ② Connecting the printer

It won't have escaped your notice that one, or maybe two, hunks of hardware are currently lying dormant on your desk or workstation. Now that you've had some practice with the mouse, keyboard and Windows itself, it's time to hook up the printer.

No two printers share exactly the same setup routine, so you may have to interpret the following pictures and directions to suit. In particular, if you have opted for a laser printer rather than an inkjet printer, you will install a single toner cartridge instead of separate ink cartridges. As always, follow the printer manual's instructions closely. Or, if it's written in the worst kind of Techno-Pidgin, toss it on the fire and trust to common sense.

We're going to work with a combined printer and scanner made by Canon. Such a device is ideal for saving space and much simpler to operate than a separate printer and scanner.

The ins and outs

For the first time, we're going to bring together hardware and the three types of software discussed on page 15.

Hardware. Pretty obvious, really – we need to connect the printer to the system unit. Printers generally use either a *parallel* cable or, much more commonly now, a USB cable. The latter is the case here. Note that printer manufacturers often fail to include a cable in the box – an unpardonable omission, in our opinion, that may see you scurrying down to your computer superstore before you can go any further.

Windows. Depending upon the make, model and age of your printer, Windows may or may not recognise the printer automatically. In other words, it may just work and it may just not. Why?

Driver. It all hinges on whether Windows has a built-in copy of the necessary driver software. Remember, a driver helps a computer make sense of its hardware components. If Windows is lacking, no matter – you will find the driver you need on a CD-ROM supplied with the printer.

Program. Click the Print button in any program and whatever you see on screen – a letter, say, or a full-colour digital image – materialises on paper. It's as simple as that. A printer without any programs to keep it busy is a dull thing indeed. Moreover, many printers ship with extra programs that let you design greetings cards, t-shirt transfers and so forth.

Unpacking and setting up

With lots of moving parts, printers are vulnerable to damage during transit. This is why they usually arrive trussed up like oven-ready turkeys. Your first task is to extract the device from its polystyrene shell, dig out the manual and unpeel all the sticky tape. Next, attach any supplied paper input and output trays or feeders. Now pause and follow the instructions very carefully indeed. You might be told to plug the printer straight into the system unit, switch it on and see what happens; or you might have a couple of other preparatory steps to complete first.

Installing the printer

Windows 7 is pretty clever when it comes to printers. If you've got a USB printer, then installing it can be as simple as switching on your PC, plugging the USB cable into a spare USB port and waiting a few seconds for Windows to recognise it. However, modern printers are capable of lots of clever things and Windows doesn't necessarily know how to use the most useful features. That's why most printers come with a CD of software: the CD contains the necessary bits and bobs that enable you to get the most from your machine.

In most cases you should install the software before you connect the printer. However, some printer manufacturers need you to connect the printer before you install the software. If you do things the wrong way round, you might encounter problems, so it makes sense to get it right first time. You'll find details of the method the manufacturer wants you to use in the printer's Quick Start guide.

In this example, our Canon printer requires us to install the software before connecting the printer. Your setup routine will be different to this but the same principles apply.

Switch on your computer and put the printer installation disc in the DVD drive. It should start automatically. If it doesn't, double click the Computer icon on your Desktop (or click Computer in the Start menu) and look for the DVD drive. Double click this icon to launch the printer installation program.

We're asked for some basic information, including location and language. Work your way through any such screens.

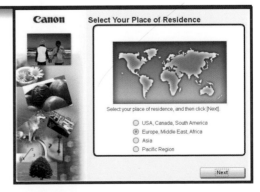

This is what we like to see – a nice, big, easy installation option!

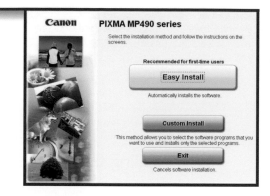

Now we are shown a list of programs that will be installed. Printers (and scanners) tend to come with a diverse selection of features rather than a single feature that does everything, which is unfortunate. However, just accept the default suggestions.

Easy Install

Drive C: 525094 MB free space
Total used space: 601 MB
Displays the README file:

MP Drivers	220 MB	On-screen Manual	30 MB
My Printer	10 MB	MP Navigator EX	75 MB
Easy-PhotoPrint EX	240 MB	Solution Menu	10 MB
Adobe RGB (1998)	1 MB	Easy-WebPrint EX	15 MB

*At some point in the process, you will certainly be required to accept an **end user agreement**. Read it if you wish but you have to accept it before you can continue.*

License Agreement
Canon Products

STEP 1
License Agreement
Canon Products
Adobe RGB (1998)

STEP 2
Installation

STEP 3
Setup

STEP 4
Information

Before installing Canon Products, carefully read the license agreement below.

END USER LICENSE AGREEMENT

ATTENTION: PLEASE READ THIS DOCUMENT BEFORE INSTALLING THE LICENSED SOFTWARE.

This is a license agreement between you and Canon Inc., having its place of business at 30-2 Shimomaruko 3-chome, Ohta-ku, Tokyo 146-8501, Japan ("Canon"), with respect to software and its associated electronic or online manuals, if any (the "Software") and/or text, image, graphic and other creations in digital format ("Contents Data"), which are provided to you with this End User License Agreement (Software and Contents Data hereinafter shall be referred to individually or collectively as the "Licensed Software").

If you accept the agreement, click [Yes]. If you click [No], the software installation will be canceled.

1 / 2

Back   No   Yes

Installation now continues. It may take some time. Have a cuppa.

Canon PIXMA MP490 series

My Printer

Installation progress: 25%

About 12 minutes until completion

Finally, we are prompted to connect the printer to the computer via a USB cable. Ensure that the printer is turned on first.

Take the cable and plug one end – the square end – into the printer and the other end – the flatter end – into any USB socket on your computer.

The installation program should now detect that the printer is connected and finish installing the software. You may be asked to align the printer cartridges but this is a straightforward process – just follow the prompts.

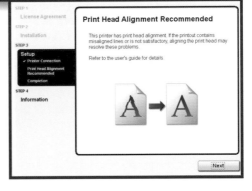

You might now be invited to register your printer with the manufacturer. This is worth doing, as you will receive updates and support. Finally, you may be asked to restart your computer – or it may work immediately without a restart.

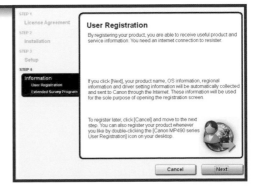

Using your printer

Any program that produces or works with anything that can be printed, such as a letter or a photograph, will now work with your printer. However, that's not quite the end of the story, as you can control the printer settings every time. Here's one example.

1

👆 *File*

👆 *Print*

👆 *OK*

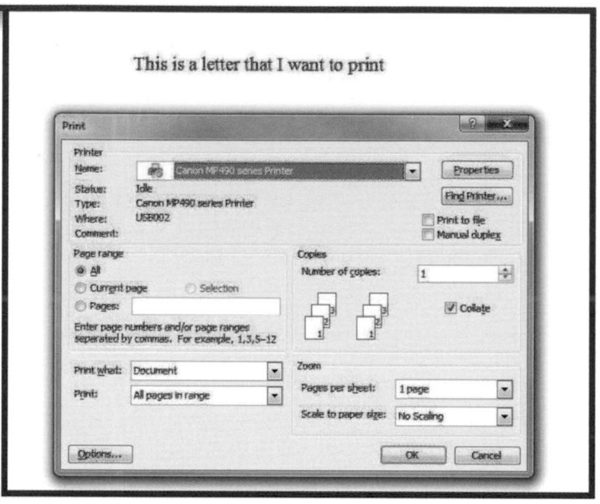

In any program, look for the Print command in the File menu. Here we want to print a letter from Microsoft Word. Make sure that your printer is selected in the Name field and click OK.

2

👆 *File*

👆 *Print*

👆 *Properties*

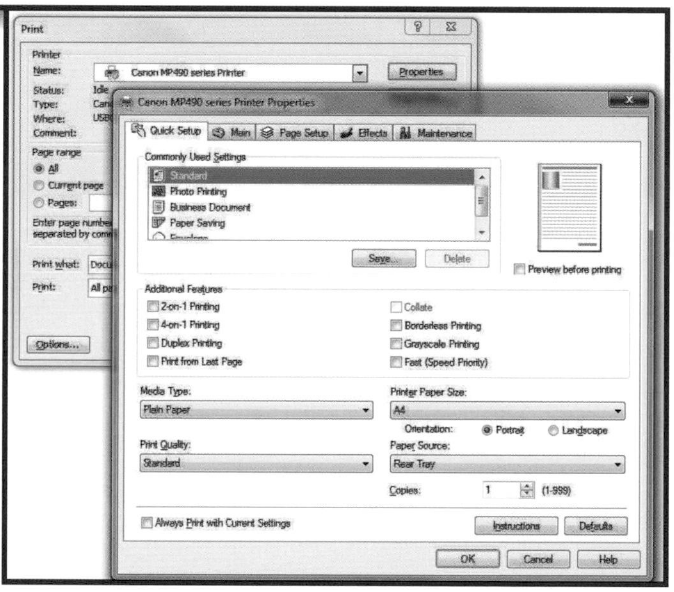

Alternatively, click the Properties button to have greater control over your printing. Your options are determined entirely by your make and model of printer, but you should be able to select the print quality (switch to top quality when printing photos but be prepared to replace your ink frequently!), change the page layout from portrait to landscape, change paper size and probably a whole host of other options. The good news is that the default settings will probably be just fine most of the time.

3

👆 *Start*

👆 *Control Panel*

👆 *View devices and printers*

👆 *[Your printer's icon]*

👆 *Display Printer Properties*

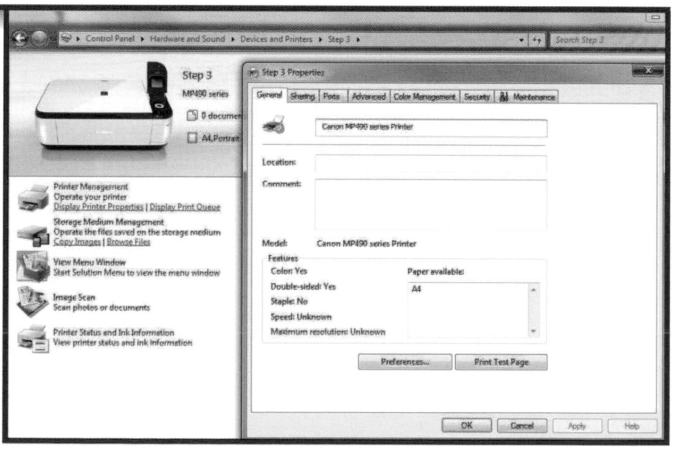

If you want to delve into the settings further, you can do this in the Control Panel. The Preferences button allows you to configure the default settings for all future printing. You might, for instance, wish to run your printer in economy mode to save on ink costs.

PART ② Scanning an image

Printers may be devilishly complex devices but scanners are comparatively simple. Essentially, a flatbed scanner – which looks like a small photocopier – takes a digital picture of whatever you place under the lid. This picture is then transferred to your computer, whereupon you can view and tweak it with an image-editing program. It needs no routine maintenance beyond an occasional wipe with a cloth, no refills and should serve you well for years.

There are other types of scanner, notably handheld devices that you pass over a page, but flatbeds are the norm for home use.

A scanner takes digital pictures that can be imported into programs and saved as files on your computer's hard disk.

Using your scanner

Installing a scanner is the same as installing a printer, only simpler because you don't have to worry about ink or toner. All scanners use the USB interface so just follow the instructions, install the software provided, and connect your scanner when told to do so. Now let's do something useful with it.

*Every scanner comes with its own scanning software, and while the programs do the same job they all do it in slightly different ways. For this walkthrough we'll use Google's free Picasa program (**www.picasa.google.com**). This is worth **downloading** even if you already have scanning software, as it's a great photo organiser too.*

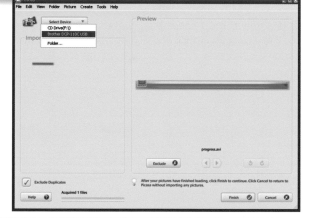

Click Import and you'll be taken to the Import screen. The first thing we need to do is to tell Picasa where to get our scan from, so click the Select Device button and choose your scanner from the drop-down. In this example we're using a Brother USB printer/scanner.

*No matter what scanner you use, you'll now see the scanning dialog. We're going to scan a colour picture, so make sure that the Color Picture button is **checked**. The next step is to do a quick preview scan to make sure everything's okay.*

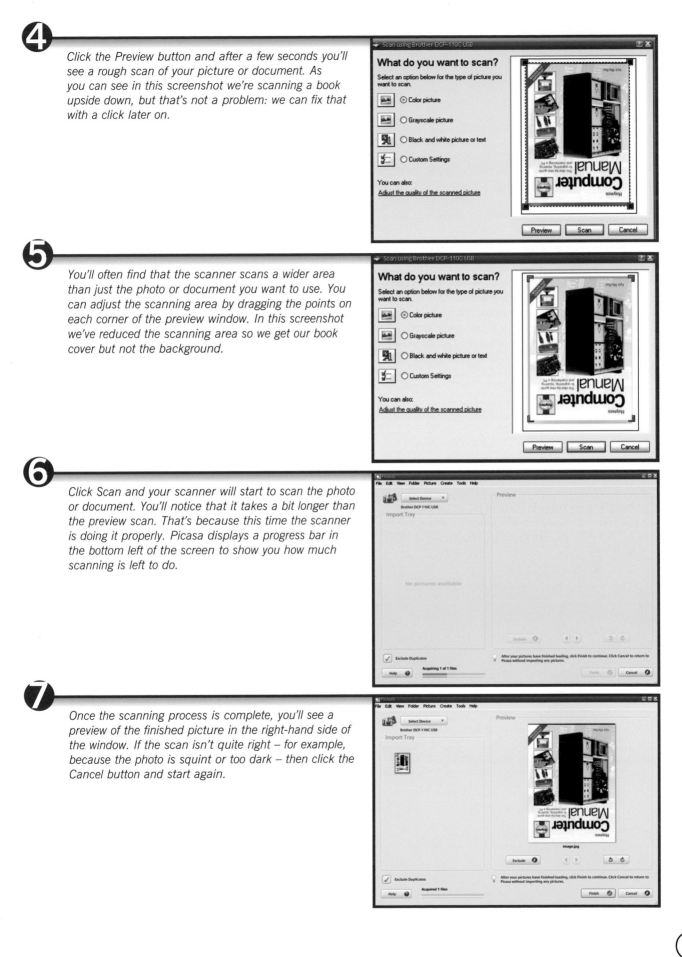

4 Click the Preview button and after a few seconds you'll see a rough scan of your picture or document. As you can see in this screenshot we're scanning a book upside down, but that's not a problem: we can fix that with a click later on.

5 You'll often find that the scanner scans a wider area than just the photo or document you want to use. You can adjust the scanning area by dragging the points on each corner of the preview window. In this screenshot we've reduced the scanning area so we get our book cover but not the background.

6 Click Scan and your scanner will start to scan the photo or document. You'll notice that it takes a bit longer than the preview scan. That's because this time the scanner is doing it properly. Picasa displays a progress bar in the bottom left of the screen to show you how much scanning is left to do.

7 Once the scanning process is complete, you'll see a preview of the finished picture in the right-hand side of the window. If the scan isn't quite right – for example, because the photo is squint or too dark – then click the Cancel button and start again.

8 As we mentioned earlier, scanning upside-down isn't a problem. If you look below and to the right of the preview image, you'll see two rotate buttons. The leftmost one rotates the image 90 degrees to the left; the rightmost, to the right. So to turn your image the right way up it's just a matter of clicking one of the rotate buttons twice.

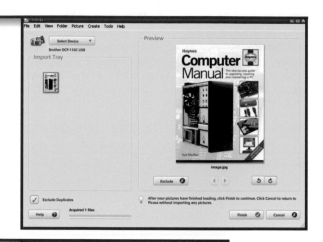

9 When you click the Finish button, Picasa will create a new folder for your image, and it will ask you to give that folder a name. If you wish you can also add additional details to remind you when you did the scan, or why you were scanning it, or you can leave those sections blank. Click Finish to continue.

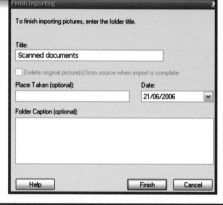

10 Picasa will now take you to the main program window, with your new scan in pride of place. You'll see that there's a toolbar at the bottom of the screen, but it's faded out: click your scan in the main window and the toolbar will come to life.

11 The toolbar enables you to carry out basic image tasks: giving your image a label, printing it out, e-mailing it or exporting it to another folder. You can also rotate your image, or use the slider at the top right of the toolbar to zoom in or out. However, if you double click your image you'll get to see the fun stuff.

12

Double clicking an image in Picasa keeps the toolbar at the bottom but opens a new one on the left-hand side of the screen. From this toolbar you can straighten wonky scans, get rid of redeye from photos, or adjust the brightness and contrast to make a scan clearer.

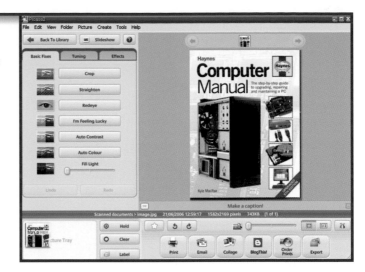

13

Picasa also enables you to add special effects: click the Effects tab and you'll see a range of options including Sharpen, Filtered B&W, Glow, Sepia and so on. To apply an effect just click it and the main image will update; in this screenshot, we've used a sepia effect to make our image look as if it's very old.

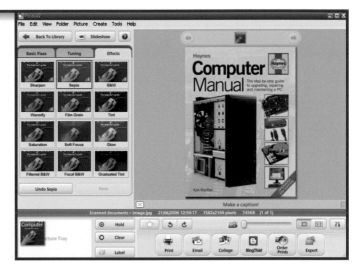

14

If you wish, you can now export your image from Picasa for use in other programs. The Image Size options are particularly handy, because high-resolution scans can take up lots of disc space. If you're planning to e-mail a picture, it's a good idea to reduce the size of your picture with the 'Resize To' slider.

PART **3**

Windows 7

As we remarked earlier, Windows is a graphical, point-and-clicky, touchy-feely kind of operating system. The upshot is that once you've mastered a few simple concepts, your computer becomes remarkably easy to use. Almost regardless of what you want to do, the same rules and steps apply.

PART **3** Key concepts

Windows typically provides ten ways to do anything and is loaded with smart shortcuts and time-saving tricks. But that way lies complexity and confusion. Here we stick to the most logical and straightforward, if not necessarily the quickest, methods of getting from A to B.

The Desktop

When you turn on your computer and Windows starts, your starting point is always the Desktop. The key areas are these:

Icons

Clickable links to programs and folders. In this example, there are five on view, but your computer's Desktop may look rather different depending on how your supplier has customised your system. Note that if you point at an icon without clicking, you'll get a pop-up bubble with a little information about it. This is called a screen tip.

Documents *A folder on the hard disk used to store files that you create when you work with programs. You can also access all other folders from here.*

Computer *A quick way to find information about your computer's hardware, including its drives.*

Network *Only relevant if your computer is linked to other computers or connected to the internet (as it will be in Part 4).*

Internet Explorer *A web browser. That is to say, the program that you'll use to view web pages on the internet.*

Recycle Bin *An important one. When you delete a file from your computer's hard disk, instead of disappearing irretrievably it actually gets stored in the Recycle Bin. This effectively gives you a chance to recover any file deleted by mistake – and believe us, you'll delete plenty of files by mistake as you work with your computer!*

Background *Just a picture to brighten up your day. In fact, it can be any picture you like.*

The Start Menu *See page 66 for a detailed description of this important item.*

Taskbar A strip running across the bottom of the screen that shows you what's going on. At the far left, we find the Start button, which we'll consider in detail in a moment. At the far right is the Notification Area which shows which programs are working quietly in the *background*. The central part of the Taskbar is used to display buttons that relate to current activity.

Desktop delights

Your Desktop is a very useful working space on which you can save files and folders and from which you can launch programs. Here's a run through of just some of the things you can do with it.

👆 *Start*

⌨ *Calculator [in the Search panel]*

👆 *Calculator*

👆 *Send To*

👆 *Desktop (create shortcut)*

To save yourself having to go through the Start menu to find programs that you use frequently, you can make shortcuts on the Desktop. Thereafter, just double-click your new shortcut to launch the program.

👆 *Desktop*

👆 *View*

👆 *Large icons*

By default, Windows displays Desktop icons in a medium size. However, you can set them to be small or large here. If you uncheck Show Desktop icons, they'll disappear completely. Reverse this to bring them back again.

👆 *Desktop*

👆 *View*

👆 *Auto arrange icons*

Again by default, Windows arranges icons in neat columns. If you uncheck the auto arrange feature, you can drag and drop them wherever you like on the Desktop.

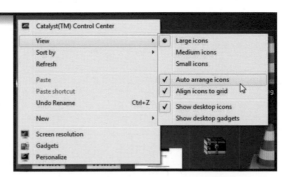

Show Desktop button

The little vertical strip at the far end of the Taskbar allows you to instantly minimise all open windows and return to the Desktop. This is handy when your boss walks in and you're in the middle of playing a computer game.

 Desktop

 Personalize

 Desktop Background

Not happy with your Desktop background, or 'wallpaper'? You can change it here. Simply select an alternative picture and click Save changes. You can use the Browse button to select one of your own pictures.

 Desktop

 Personalize

You can change the overall appearance of Windows 7 by selecting a new theme. Your computer manufacturer might have installed one or more of its own themes but you should find some alternatives in the Aero Themes section. The Landscape theme is particularly striking.

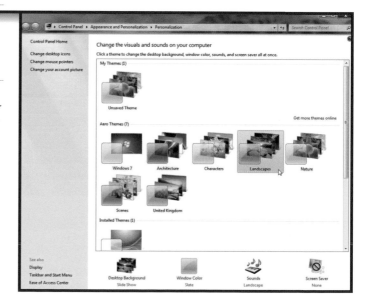

Taskbar tricks

The Taskbar remains visible on screen even when the Desktop is completely covered by windows. Its most obvious and useful function is to allow you to switch between windows and between programs. Let's see this in action.

🖱️ *Start*

⌨️ *Notepad [in the Search panel]*

🖱️ *Notepad*

This launches the Notepad program. Note that a new icon appears in the Taskbar. Click this icon, or button, and Notepad will minimise. That is, the program will disappear from the Desktop. Click it again and Notepad will reappear. Leave Notepad running for now.

🖱️ *Start*

⌨️ *Calculator [in the Search panel]*

🖱️ *Calculator*

Now launch the Calculator program. You should now have two icons in the Taskbar – Notepad and Calculator. Click on the icons to switch between the programs. You can have them both running at the same time, both minimised or any other combination.

Windows 7 has a nifty feature called Aero Peek. Try pointing at the Notepad icon (or Calculator icon) in the Taskbar but don't click. You'll see a popup window that shows you the program. This window is 'live' in the sense that it shows you what's going on in the program at the time.

The Start Menu

You could sit and stare at the Desktop all day but to do something useful you need the Start button and its corresponding menu. Click it once and you'll see something like this. What can it all mean?

Pinned Programs *This section contains fixed links to certain programs. This means that you can always access them directly from the Start menu. To add a program here, right click its icon in the Start menu and select Pin to Start menu.*

Recently Opened Programs *This section updates all the time to reflect the programs that you use most, aside from any in the Pinned Programs section. Note the little arrow to the right of the program icons. If you click this arrow, you'll see a list of the files most recently opened with that program – this is another useful shortcut, called a 'jump list'.*

All Programs *Click here to access a full list of all the programs installed on your computer. As you install more and more software on your computer, you'll begin to see the attraction of the Pinned Programs and Recently Opened Programs sections of the Start menu. They provide useful shortcuts to the programs that you use most often and save you always having to root through the All Programs list.*

Search *We've already used this a few times. The Search box allows you to type in the name of any program or file on your computer in order to find it quickly.*

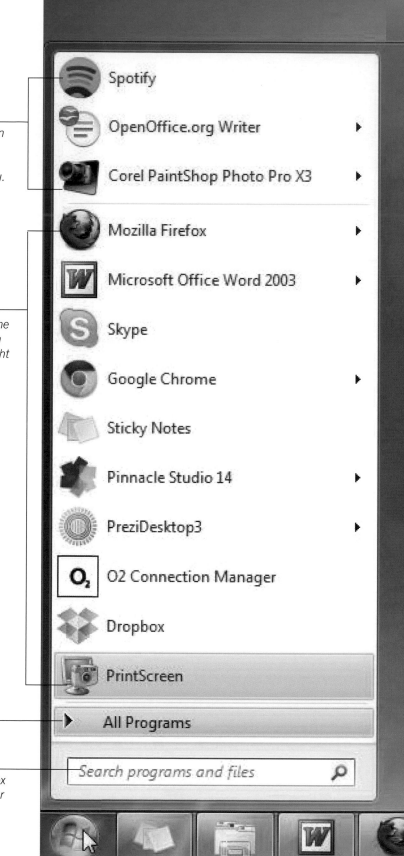

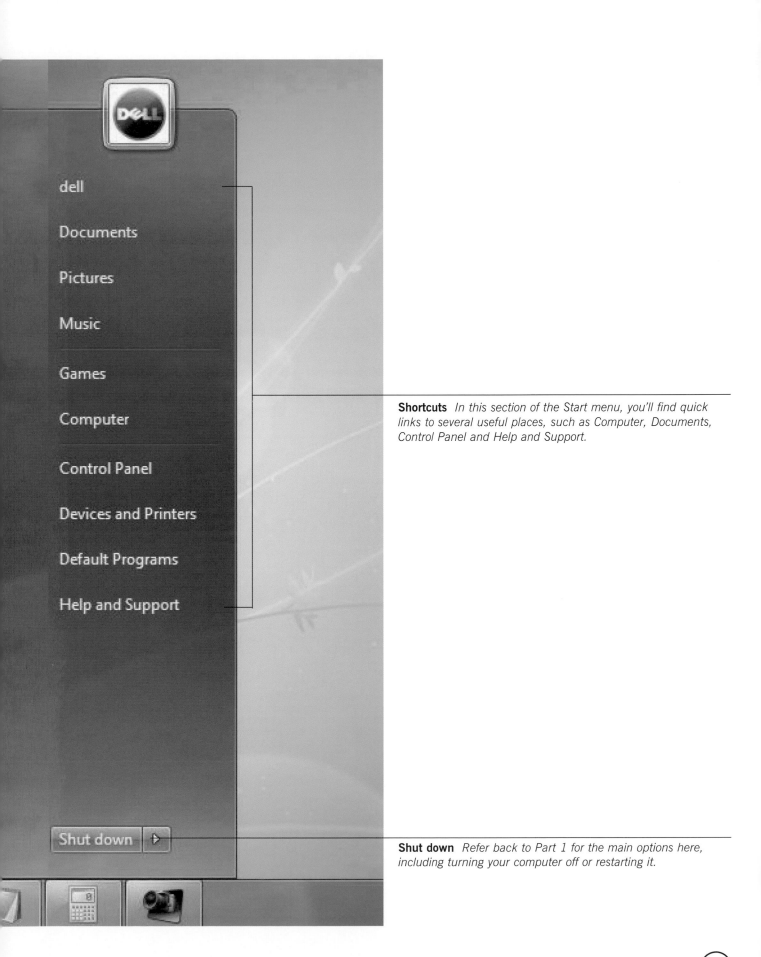

dell

Documents

Pictures

Music

Games

Computer

Control Panel

Devices and Printers

Default Programs

Help and Support

Shut down ▷

Shortcuts *In this section of the Start menu, you'll find quick links to several useful places, such as Computer, Documents, Control Panel and Help and Support.*

Shut down *Refer back to Part 1 for the main options here, including turning your computer off or restarting it.*

Getting comfortable with windows

Whenever you open a program or perform a task on your computer, the action takes place inside a self-contained box on your monitor screen called a window. Each open window is (more or less) independent of all others and, as we have seen, you can switch between windows using the Taskbar. Here we look at two typical windows' key features.

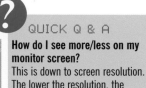

QUICK Q & A

How do I see more/less on my monitor screen?
This is down to screen resolution. The lower the resolution, the bigger everything appears but the less room you have for lots of windows; increase the resolution and windows and icons shrink, but you can squeeze more onto the screen at any one time. Consult your monitor's manual to check which resolutions it 'supports' (i.e. can work with), and experiment here:

- Desktop
- Screen resolution
- Change the resolution
- Apply
- OK

QUICK Q & A

I'm never sure when I'm supposed to single click or double click, and it's driving me mad!
It's a fair point. As a rule, double clicking launches a program or a window from an icon, and single clicking works when it's an entry on a list or menu (e.g. the Start menu). On the internet, you only ever need to single click **hyperlinks**. If you'd prefer to do away with double-clicking altogether, try this:

- Start
- Folder Options [in the Search panel]
- Single click to open an item
- Apply
- OK

Title bar The shaded top edge of a window displays the name of the program or process. The title bar also has three important little buttons.

The first minimises the window i.e. turns it into a button on the Taskbar. To restore it, you click the Taskbar button.

The middle button maximises the window so that it takes up all available screen space. Click it again to restore the window to its original size.

The final button closes the window.

You can also click any point on the title bar, hold down the mouse button, drag the window to a different position on the screen and then drop it in place. Don't forget that you can resize windows too (see page 32).

Menu bar A number of clickable menus containing organised control and configuration options. The contents of each menu depends upon the program or process.

Scrollbar When it's not possible to see the entire contents of a window all at one time, a scrollbar appears. This lets you scroll up and down and through the window. Either click and drag the scrollbar slider or click the little arrows above and below the scrollbar (or to the left and right, in the case of a horizontal scrollbar).

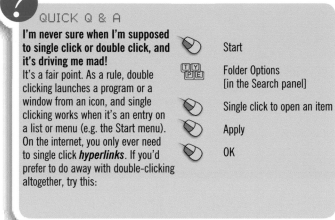

A Windows Explorer window

Toolbar Some options that you may need when working in the window. For instance, the New Folder button allows you to create a new folder within Documents with one click. These tools vary depending upon what window you have open.

Search Here you can type the name of any file you want to find. By default, the search looks through the contents of the current window. Because we have the Documents window open, a search will look for files within the Documents folder and sub-folders (folders within folders).

Address bar Windows 7 adopts a 'breadcrumbs' approach to navigation. In this example, the Documents folder is located within an upper folder called Libraries. You can work backwards through a hierarchy of folders by clicking the breadcrumb navigation.

Pane A window may be sub-divided into separate sections. Each section is, predictably enough, called a window pane.

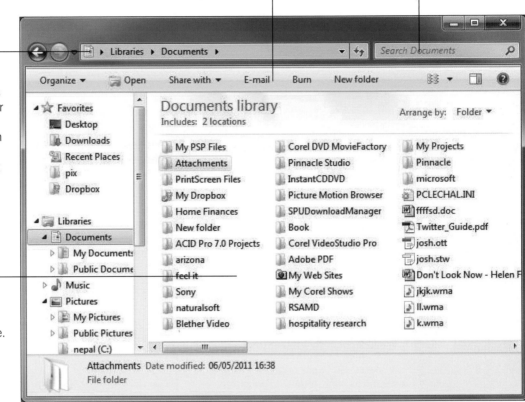

Some ways with windows

Windows 7 has some cool ways of manipulating windows. If you drag a window to one side of the screen, it will 'snap' into place and fill exactly half of the screen horizontally. Do the same on the other side with a different window and it will fill the other half. This makes it easy to work with two windows side-by-side.

If you have several windows open but you only want to work with one, try clicking on the title bar and 'shaking' it from side to side. All other windows will minimise, leaving only the current window open on the Desktop.

Snap windows into place side-by-side by dragging them to one side of the screen.

The Windows Control Panel

The Windows Control Panel is a wonderful thing: with it you can change almost everything Windows does, from the way it looks to the way it performs. In this section, we discover the key Control Panel components that can make your system sing.

To go to the Control Panel, click on the Start menu and choose Control Panel from the list at the right. You should now see a screen like this one. The Control Panel has many, many features, organised within a few main sections.

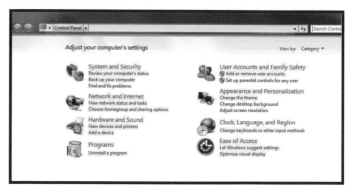

System and Security *Here's where you look after the computer's wellbeing. Click the System and Security link and have a browse through the menus. Be sure to check the Windows Update section. By default, Windows 7 will automatically download and install important security updates and you should ensure that the 'Install updates automatically' option is activated.*

Windows Experience Index *Click the link to Check the Windows Experience Index in the System menu. This tool gives your computer a score of between 1.0 and 7.9 based on its hardware and software configuration. If your computer has a score of, say, 5.0 you can install any software that requires a score of 5.0 or less (check the box for details).*

Windows Firewall *A firewall is a security measure that prevents malicious software from accessing your computer through the internet. We'll look at this in more detail in Part 4. For now, check that the Windows Firewall is turned on. It should be, but check!*

4

Action Center *Pay a visit to the Action Center. In the Maintenance section, you may find some messages relating to known issues. If you see a 'Check for solution' button, give this a click and see if Microsoft can fix things.*

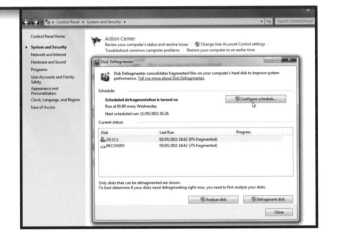

5

Disk Defragmenter *Click the 'Defragment your hard drive' link. You won't need to defragment your hard drive immediately if you've just set up a new computer but over time it's wise to do so weekly. You can set up an automatic schedule by clicking the Configure schedule button. See our note at the foot of page 73 for more.*

6

Display *Return to the Control Panel and click Hardware and Sound. Now look for the Display link and click this. One very useful option is the ability to make text and other items larger or smaller. You have three choices – smaller, medium or larger. If you struggle to see items on screen, especially if you have eyesight problems, try switching from smaller to medium or larger. It can make a huge difference.*

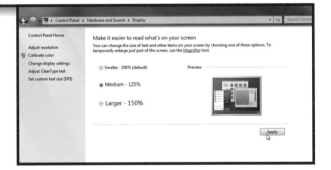

7

Sound *Look for the Adjust system volume link in the Sound menu. This controls the initial volume of your speakers. If you struggle to hear music or other sounds, turn it up a bit here. If your speakers are deafening, turn the volume down instead!*

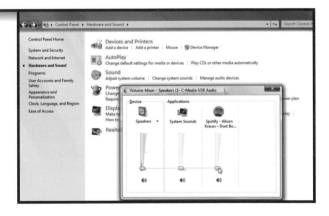

8

Power Options *Look for Power Options and click Change power-saving settings. If a plan is already selected, click Change plan settings. Here you can decide when your monitor turns itself off and when, if at all, your computer goes to 'sleep' (both useful options for saving power). We suggest turning off the monitor after 10 minutes of inactivity. Personally we prefer to avoid automatic sleeping and recommend just turning off your computer when you're finished using it.*

9

Appearance and Personalization *We've already glanced at changing the screen resolution, background picture and Windows theme. In this section, all the main tools are gathered together. The Ease of Access Center is worth a visit if you have any difficulties with your vision. For instance, the Magnifier tool enlarges areas of the screen to make them easier to read.*

10

Desktop Gadgets *A 'gadget' is a program that runs right on your Desktop, all the time. You'll either love them or hate them. If, for instance, you want to have a large clock or a localised weather forecast within easy view on your Desktop, click Add gadgets to the Desktop and double click any that take your fancy.*

11

Network and Internet *Now return to the Control Panel and enter the Network and Internet section, followed by Network and Sharing Center. If you have already set up your internet connection, you should see it here. If not, read Part 4 when you're ready. Make a note of the 'Troubleshoot problems' link, as you may need this one day if your internet connection plays up or goes down.*

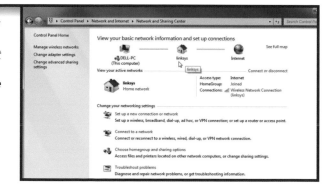

Internet Options *Back up to Network and Internet and click the Internet Options link. This opens a window that allows you to configure how your web browser handles internet content. Click the Privacy tab and ensure that the main setting is Medium (the default).*

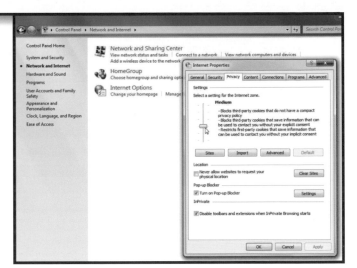

Do I need to worry about the Control Panel?

Quite possibly not. You may well have years of pain-free computer use without ever having to look for and tweak these and other settings. However, you should know how to find the Control Panel and we recommend that you explore the menus and features. If and when you run into unexpected problems, the Control Panel is likely to help you.

We also suggest that you explore Windows Help and Support. You'll find a link to this on the Start menu near the Control Panel link. If you have an issue, search for help here.

Why 'defragging' can speed up your PC

When Windows saves a file, it breaks it into bits and stores those bits in different places – which is a good thing, because it's designed to make the best use of the available storage. However, these days even the humblest PC has a massive hard disk and the more widely spread a file becomes, the more time it takes to find the various pieces of a file when Windows needs it. Individually the delay is tiny, but if you have thousands of files on your PC – which you do, because Windows alone consists of thousands of individual files – then, as your files become more widely spread, the delays add up to cause a noticeable drop in performance.

The answer is defragmentation, or 'defragging' as it's often called. When you defrag your hard disk, the individual bits of files scattered around your hard disk are brought closer together – which means Windows has to spend less time looking for them and your system speeds up as a result. You don't need to defragment very often, but if you think your PC is getting a bit sluggish then defragging your hard disk could solve the problem.

Windows Help and Support

display

Best 30 results for display

1. Calibrate your display
2. Getting the best display on your monitor
3. Install or change a display language
4. Ways to improve display quality
5. How do I get additional display languages?
6. Conserving battery power
7. How do I make the display on my laptop brighter?
8. Adjust your monitor's brightness and contrast
9. Change the display of dates, times, currency, and measurements
10. Display native digit systems
11. Display Hijiri dates
12. Use the computer without a display
13. Correct monitor flicker (refresh rate)
14. Switch between display modes in Windows Media Player
15. Change how you view a Journal note
16. Desktop gadgets (overview)
17. Move windows between multiple monitors
18. Change how you display items in the Windows Media Player Library

More support options

Online Help

PART 3 Files and folders

Sooner or later, you're going to create something on your computer that you want to save. You have a choice of storage locations, as we'll see in the very next section, but first it helps to get a handle on the notion of files and folders – and, specifically, how Windows works with them.

Here we see some individual files – every photo is a file – and three folders. Your computer can store files within folders and folders within folders.

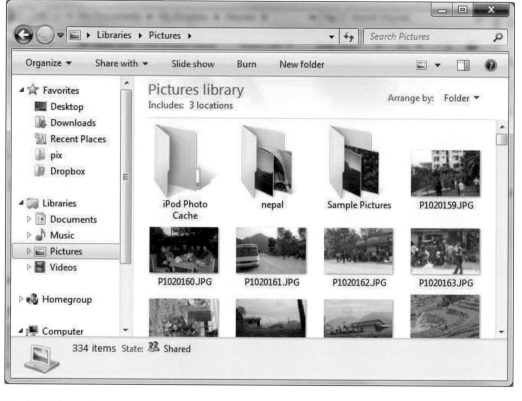

So what's a file?

A file is any single self-contained chunk of information stored in a digital format. A letter written on a word processor and saved to the hard disk is a file; an image created on or copied from a scanner or a digital camera is a file; a computer-generated sound recording is a file; a digital video clip is a file; even a computer program is a file (or, rather, a collection of files).

Although all files are essentially just a collection of 1s and 0s – that is, *binary data* – your computer has to be able to tell one file from another. Thus every file has two parts: a file name, and a file extension that tells the computer something about its format. When you make your own files, you choose the name as you go along, and you can be as creative or pedantic as you like. The extension, however, ties the file to a particular program or type of program, and needs to be chosen with care (when indeed there is a choice at all). An extension is usually 2, 3 or 4 letters long and tacked on to the file name proper with a dot separating them.

For example, let's say you write a letter in Word, the popular word processing program, and call it 'Hi Mum'. Word's default file extension is '.doc', so this file's full title becomes 'Hi Mum.doc'. Now, any other computer with a recent version of Word

installed can open, read and edit this file. You will, of course, be able to open it yourself whenever you like.

Some file formats and their associated extensions are proprietary. The '.doc' format belongs to Microsoft, for instance, which effectively means that only Word and other Microsoft programs can create or open '.doc' files. (Actually, some other word processors can work with '.doc' files but only by means of special import filters.)

However, many file formats are non-proprietary, which means that they are compatible with a wider range of programs. A sound recording, for instance, might be saved in the common .wav format and opened with just about any program capable of playing sound files. A web page – which is, after all, just another file – will generally have an .htm or .html extension, and any web browser the world over can view it.

The only time you really have to worry about file formats and extensions is when you want to share your files. That is, if you write a report in Word and save it with the '.doc' file extension, you should first ensure that all intended recipients of the file have a copy of Word on their computers. Failing that, you can choose an alternative non-proprietary file extension. In the case of text files, this would generally be '.txt' or '.rtf'.

OK, so what's a folder?

A folder is a file holder. Just as you might keep your paper documents in a series of folders in a filing cabinet, so on a computer you save files in the virtual equivalent of folders. A folder is just an organisational tool – a gimmick, if you like – designed to make file management intuitive and sensible.

Moreover, Windows lets you work with a hierarchy of 'nested' files and folders (i.e. files within folders within folders within folders, and so on, more or less forever). The advantage is that you can organise your work in such a way that it's easy to retrieve any individual file in moments. When you consider that your computer's hard disk can easily hold *millions* of files, good file management is truly essential.

Say you write a letter to your bank manager on your computer, print out a hard copy and post it. You're going to want to keep a copy on your computer, and that means saving the letter as a file. But where, exactly? Let's imagine that you already have a folder called Home Finances. This sounds like a good starting point. However, you also keep details of household bills and standing orders and hire purchase agreements in here. What you need is a subfolder within Home Finances called something like Bank Correspondence. Now *that* would be a good place to store your letter. Even if you completely forget where you've saved it, you should be able to track it down months or even years down the line.

But where do all these folders come from? The answer is that you make them yourself as you go along. It's time for some practical exercises.

Making folders

Here we create a brand new folder on your computer's hard disk.

Start menu

Documents

Windows provides a very useful 'top-level' folder called Documents. You might find its icon on the Desktop (in which case, double click to open the folder) or definitely in the Start menu. Inside Documents, you may find several other folders. What you will not find is a folder called Home Finances. So let's make one now.

2

🖱 *New folder*

This option is found near the top of the Documents window. Click it.

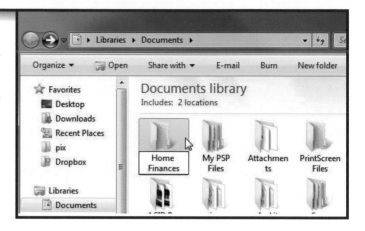

3

⌨ *Home Finances* [Enter]

---

*The default name for a new folder is, unsurprisingly, New folder. However, because the words 'New folder' are automatically highlighted at the point of creating the folder, all you have to do is **overtype** a new title. In this case, we're calling it Home Finances. Press the Enter key to save the change.*

4

🖱 *New folder*

🖱 *Rename*

⌨ *Home Finances* [Enter]

This step only applies if Step 3 goes wrong and you didn't manage to rename the folder while 'New folder' was highlighted. Right click your new folder and select Rename from the menu that appears. Now just type Home Finances and press the Enter key. Any folder can be renamed at any time in this manner.

5

🖱 *Home Finances*

🖱 *New Folder*

⌨ *Bank Correspondence* [Enter]

We now want to create a subfolder within Home Finances called Bank Correspondence. Double click the Home Finances folder icon to open the folder (which is, of course, currently empty). Now create and name a new folder just as in Steps 2 and 3 above. Once again, you can easily rename the folder as in Step 4 if anything goes wrong.

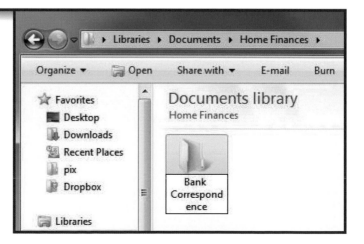

Saving and opening files

You now have a suitable home for a letter to your bank manager. What you do not yet have is the letter itself, so let's create and save just such a file now.

1

🖱️ *Start*

⌨️ *WordPad [in the Search panel]*

🖱️ *WordPad*

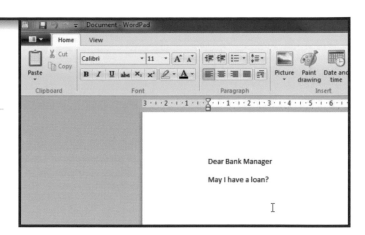

Yes, it's back to trusty WordPad again. There's every chance that your computer system came with a fully-fledged word processor like Microsoft Word but this will do for now. Open the program and type a letter to your bank manager. Or rather, to save time, type anything you like, even just a word or two.

2

🖱️ *File*

🖱️ *Save As*

In some ways, this is the most important lesson in the entire manual. What you're about to do is save a file. Once saved, this file – any file – will be stored safely on your computer's hard disk. But until it is saved, the file doesn't really exist. A sudden power cut would obliterate it.

You'll find the File menu option on the far left of the menu bar. Click it once and down drops a dropdown menu. Move the mouse pointer down through the menu until Save As is highlighted and then click once.

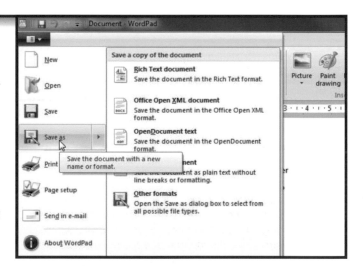

3

🖱️ *Documents*

🖱️🖱️ *Home Finances*

The Save As window is where you pick a location for your file. Look in the left-hand side of the Save As window for Documents and click. All the folders within Documents will appear in the main window pane. Double click Home Finances to open this folder.

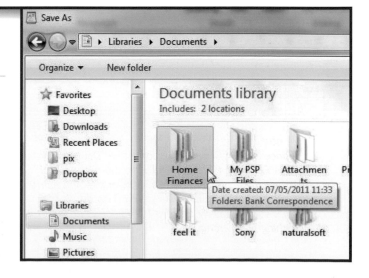

4

Bank Correspondence

You should now see your Bank Correspondence sub-folder in the Home Finances folder. Double click it to open the folder.

5

File name box

Letter to bank manager [Enter]

Save

You have navigated successfully to the Bank Correspondence folder, which is where your file will now be saved. In the File name box near the bottom of the window, type a name for your file. Click the Save button when you're finished.

6

[Change the text]

[Close button]

The Save As window disappears and you're back with your document again. Check the window's title bar and you'll see that it displays your chosen file name – proof that your file saving has been successful. Now make some small change to the letter, such as adding or deleting a word or two. Now try to close the window by clicking the red cross button in the top right.

7

Save

WordPad identifies that the file you are trying to close is not the same in every respect as the file you originally saved. This means that the original file is about to be overwritten by (that is, deleted and replaced with) this amended version, so the program asks you whether this is indeed what you intend. It's a crucial point: if you click Don't Save, the changes you just made will be lost and the file will revert to its original form; click Save and the amended file will be saved and the original one lost. In this case, click Save. The file will close.

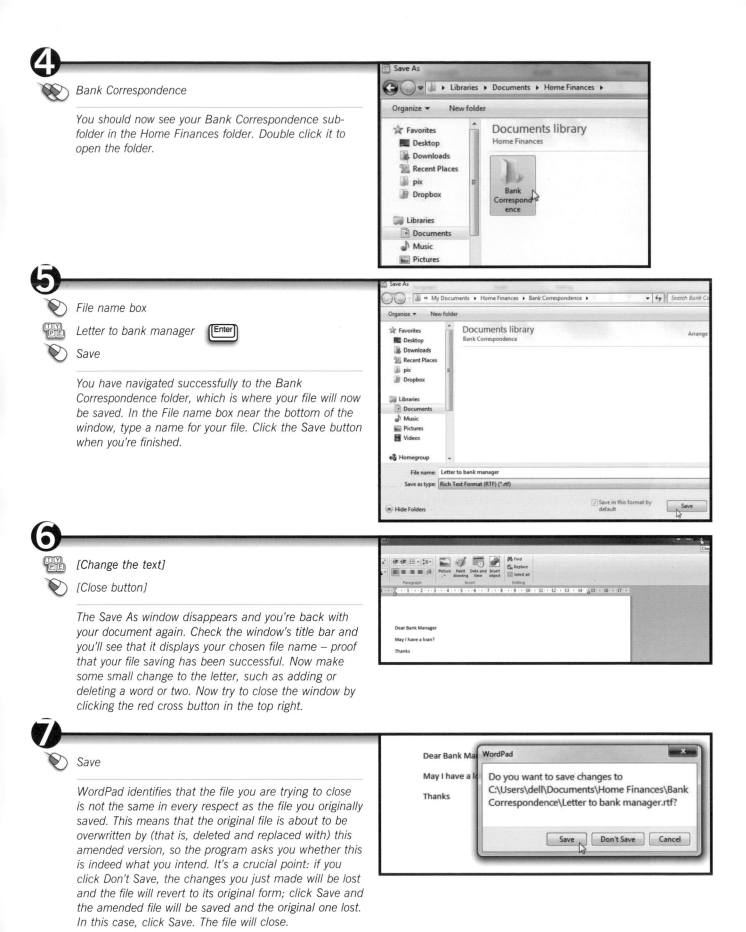

8

👆 *Start*

⌨ *WordPad [in the Search panel]*

👆 *WordPad*

👆 *File*

👆 *Open*

Let's now suppose that you wish to find and read this file at some later date. We'll show you two ways to go about this. First, launch WordPad and click Open from the File menu.

9

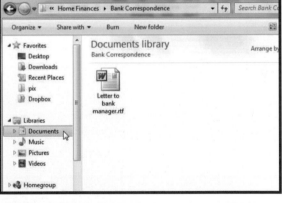

👆 *Documents*

👆 *Home Finances*

👆 *Bank Correspondence*

👆 *Letter to bank manager*

Now it's a case of navigating through folders until you find the letter. Click on the Documents icon to select this folder, then open your Home Finances folder and Bank Correspondence folder until you see your letter. Double click it to open the letter in WordPad.

10

👆 *Documents*

👆 *Home Finances*

👆 *Bank Correspondence*

Alternatively, you can locate and open this (or any) file through the Documents folder. Double click the Documents icon on the Desktop (or click the link in the Start menu) to open the folder in a window and then double click the Home Finances icon within it. Repeat with the Bank Correspondence folder.

11

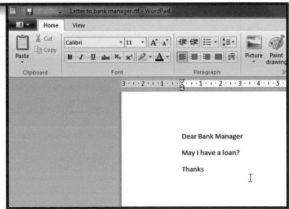

👆 *Letter to bank manager*

Finally, double click the icon that represents your file. This launches the WordPad program and opens your file simultaneously.

Deleting, recovering and searching for files. Oh, and a shortcut too.

Windows offers several ways of manipulating files and folders. Here's a run down.

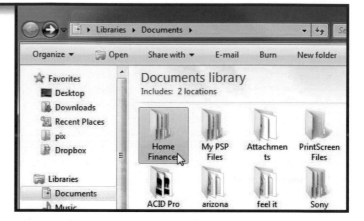

Documents

Home Finances

A single click on the Home Finances folder selects it (double clicking would open it).

Organize

Delete

Yes

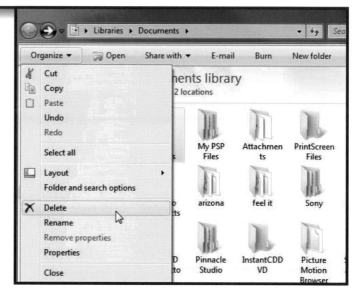

If you follow this through, you will delete your Home Finances folder and everything within it. That means that your Bank Correspondence folder and the letter to your bank manager will also be deleted (but give it a try – we'll get it back in a moment).

Recycle Bin

Home Finances

Restore this item

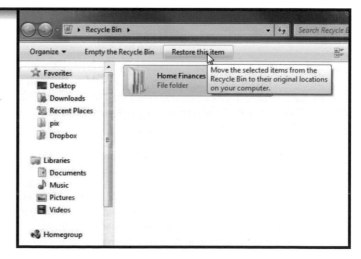

Deleting a folder or a file doesn't really erase it. It simply sends it to the Recycle Bin. Open the Recycle Bin now and find your 'deleted' Home Finances folder. Select it with a click and you can easily restore it. It will go straight back to the Documents folder.

4

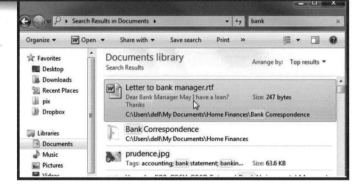

 Documents

 bank [in the search panel] [Enter]

Let's suppose that you haven't been terribly rigorous with your file management and have somehow misplaced your letter. Windows has a built-in search facility which you can access from any window (and from the Start menu, as we have seen). Just enter the name of your file if you can remember it, or even just part of the file name.

⑤

Letter to bank manager

Hey presto, there it is. The search feature in Windows 7 is extremely powerful. Double click the icon for your letter to open it in WordPad.

⑥

Documents

Home Finances

Bank Correspondence

Letter to bank manager

Send to

Desktop (create shortcut)

Finally, one time-saving tip we just can't resist. When you work with particular folders or files frequently, you can place a shortcut to them right on the Desktop. This saves you having to navigate through the Documents folder every time.

Open the Documents folder as before, find your letter and right click the icon. When the menu pops up, select Send to followed by Desktop. The original file stays where it is in the Bank Correspondence folder but now you'll find a new icon on the Desktop. This, we stress, is not the file itself but merely a shortcut, or link, to the original file. You can now open the file at any time by double clicking its Desktop icon.

Copying files and folders

You will sometimes want to move a file or a whole folder from one location on the hard disk to another. This is very easily accomplished in Windows.

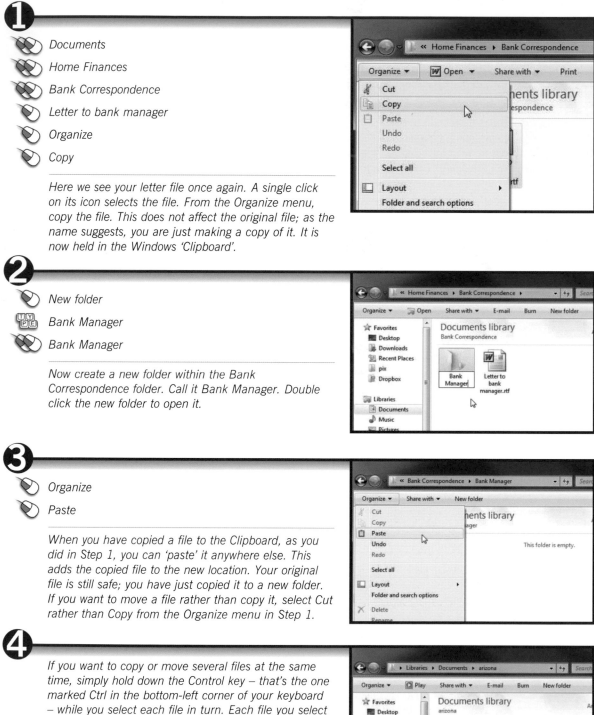

1

🖱 *Documents*

🖱 *Home Finances*

🖱 *Bank Correspondence*

🖱 *Letter to bank manager*

🖱 *Organize*

🖱 *Copy*

Here we see your letter file once again. A single click on its icon selects the file. From the Organize menu, copy the file. This does not affect the original file; as the name suggests, you are just making a copy of it. It is now held in the Windows 'Clipboard'.

2

🖱 *New folder*

⌨ *Bank Manager*

🖱 *Bank Manager*

Now create a new folder within the Bank Correspondence folder. Call it Bank Manager. Double click the new folder to open it.

3

🖱 *Organize*

🖱 *Paste*

When you have copied a file to the Clipboard, as you did in Step 1, you can 'paste' it anywhere else. This adds the copied file to the new location. Your original file is still safe; you have just copied it to a new folder. If you want to move a file rather than copy it, select Cut rather than Copy from the Organize menu in Step 1.

4

If you want to copy or move several files at the same time, simply hold down the Control key – that's the one marked Ctrl in the bottom-left corner of your keyboard – while you select each file in turn. Each file you select will be highlighted. Then use the Organize menu as in Step 1 to copy or cut the selected files.

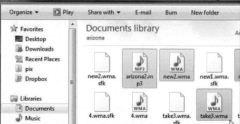

PART ③ **Working with drives**

Earlier, we discussed drives in the context of hardware. Now let's put them to work. We'll assume here that your computer has two main drives: a hard disk drive (that's a definite) and a DVD drive. It may also have a selection of additional drives designed to take memory cards.

Using Computer

On the Desktop or in the Start menu, or both, you'll find an icon for Computer. Double click it now.

 Computer

Here we see our two main drives. Note that each is assigned a drive letter appended with a colon. This is how Windows tells one drive from another. In this case, we have:

- a hard disk drive, labelled C:
- a DVD drive, labelled D:

We also have drives E:, F:, G: and H:. These are greyed out in this screenshot, which simply means that they are currently empty. Each of these four additional drives is just a slot in the case into which you can slide a removable memory card from a digital camera or other portable device.

Hard disk drive

In normal use, you won't need to visit Computer at all. You're interested in your files and folders and you get to them through the Documents link (you can see this in the left panel in the screenshot above). However, it's worth knowing that the hard disk (C: drive) essentially 'is' your computer. It's where Windows and all installed programs live. Your computer reads data from the hard disk drive every time you launch a program or perform a task; and you save data to the hard disk drive whenever you save a file (usually within the Documents folder).

If you see an additional hard disk drive called something like Recovery Partition, leave well alone! This is really just a section of the C: drive that has been set aside to store the files required to restore your computer to its original state in the event of a fatal malfunction.

DVD drive

With older versions of Windows, recording onto a DVD disc, or even a CD, was a fraught process. Thankfully, Windows 7 makes it easy. So long as you have a relatively new computer, you won't have to worry about all the different types of DVD disc around; your DVD drive will play and record to them all.

Here's a walkthrough of how to copy files onto a blank recordable (use once) or rewriteable (use as often as you like) DVD. To get started, simply pop a blank disc into the DVD drive and close the drawer.

USB drives

USB 'flash', 'pen' or 'keyring' drives are tiny solid-state (no moving parts) drives that you plug into any USB port on any computer. You can copy files to and from such a drive without any software installation because it appears in Windows as if it were a hard disk drive. USB drives are much faster and easier to work with than DVDs and, in our opinion, a must-have investment for quick backups. Capacities range from a few dozen megabytes well into *gigabytes*, with prices rising accordingly.

Burn files to disc

When you put a blank disc in the DVD drive, Windows should offer you a menu of choices in a popup window. The precise options you see depend upon what software you have installed on your computer, but we're interested in using Windows itself – or, technically, Windows Explorer, a program within Windows – to copy files to the disc.

[A title for your DVD]

With a CD/DVD player

It's useful to label your DVD with a title, whether it's the current date or something more meaningful to you, such as 'backup copy of my novel'.

3

Windows now offers you an empty (aside from one file you can ignore) window into which you should copy the files that you want to copy onto the DVD. We did this earlier in the Files and folders section but here's a refresher. Let's say you want to make a copy of your Home Finances folder. Leave the DVD window open for now.

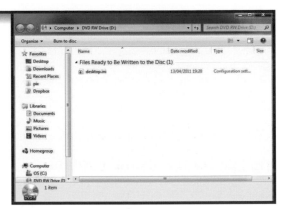

4

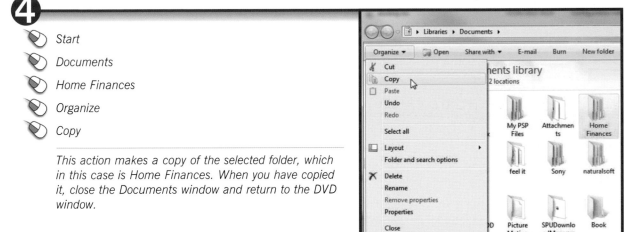

- *Start*
- *Documents*
- *Home Finances*
- *Organize*
- *Copy*

This action makes a copy of the selected folder, which in this case is Home Finances. When you have copied it, close the Documents window and return to the DVD window.

5

- *Organize*
- *Paste*

Pasting transfers a copy of the Home Finances folder to the DVD folder. It doesn't move or delete the original folder, so don't panic.

6

- *Burn to disc*
- *Next*
- *Finish*

It's as simple as that. Windows will now copy the Home Finances folder onto the blank DVD disc. When the process is complete, you'll be prompted to close the DVD window. You can now use the finished DVD disc on any other computer to access your folder. You might, for example, want to copy the folder onto a laptop.

Copying images from a digital camera

With digital cameras ubiquitous, you'll doubtless want to transfer your images onto your computer in order to save, tweak and print them. Here's how.

1

Change

Remove the memory card from your camera and push it into one of the memory card slots on your computer. You have may have three or four such slots, where each is designed for one particular type of memory card. Windows should now show you an Import Media Files window. Click the Change button.

2

My Pictures

OK

In this step, you can tell Windows where to put your photos. We recommend the My Pictures folder, which you'll find in the Pictures folder within the Libraries folder.

3

Import

That's it – Windows will now copy your photos from the memory card to the folder you nominated in Step 2. It will, in fact, create a new folder for them, using today's date as the folder name. To find them, simply open the Pictures folder from the Start menu.

PART ③ Working with programs

So far, we've worked exclusively with and within Windows. However, for all its games, features and built-in mini-programs, such as WordPad and Paint, remember that Windows is 'only' an operating system for your computer. To make the most of your hardware, you'll need some application software proper. In fact, your computer supplier almost certainly supplied a program or two as part of the deal.

Now, we can't begin to cover the ins and outs of all the different programs out there but we can show you a standard software installation and removal procedure.

Installing a program

To install a program means to copy its files from a CD, a DVD or a download to your computer's hard disk drive so you can use the program whenever you like.

If you buy your software from a shop (off the shelf), it will come in a box with a disc or two. Just pop the disc in your DVD drive and it should start automatically. Follow the prompts.

However, it's also possible, and increasingly common, to buy software from websites, in which case you'll download the program file and install it without needing a physical disc. We'll do that here with a program called Spotify, which allows you to listen to commercial music on your computer.

We're assuming that your computer has an internet connection here – see Part 4 if not. Fire up Internet Explorer and visit **www.spotify.com**. *Click the link inviting you to Try Spotify now.*

2 Create a user name and enter a password. Spotify requires you to log in to use the service.

3 Spotify now asks you for a little personal information. Be sure to check the box that signifies your acceptance of the end user agreement and click Go to the next step.

4 Now select which version of Spotify you want to use. We'll go with the free version. Click Continue. Spotify is ready to download the program to your computer. Software that doesn't require registration will start at this point. Click Download.

5 When prompted, click Save to save the installation file. Windows will ask you where you want to save the file. The default location is a folder called Downloads, which is just fine.

6

When the download is complete, click Run to install Spotify. If you are asked to confirm that you will allow Spotify to make changes to your computer, click Yes.

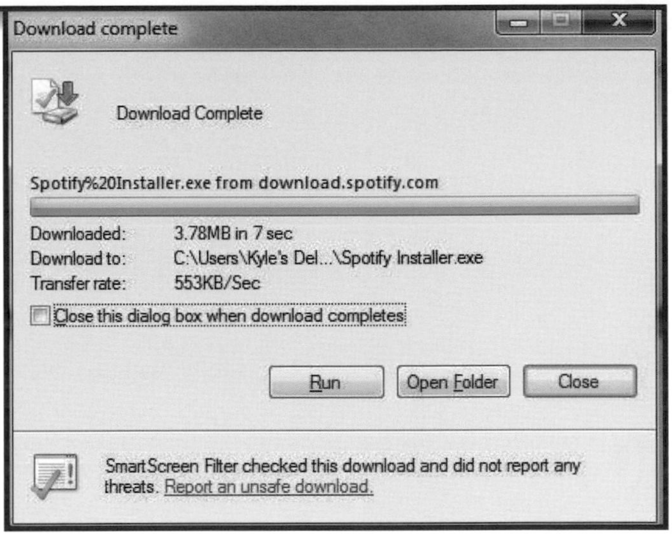

Download complete

Download Complete

Spotify%20Installer.exe from download.spotify.com

Downloaded: 3.78MB in 7 sec
Download to: C:\Users\Kyle's Del...\Spotify Installer.exe
Transfer rate: 553KB/Sec

☐ Close this dialog box when download completes

Run   Open Folder   Close

SmartScreen Filter checked this download and did not report any threats. Report an unsafe download.

7

When asked where you wish to install Spotify, accept the default suggestion and click Install.

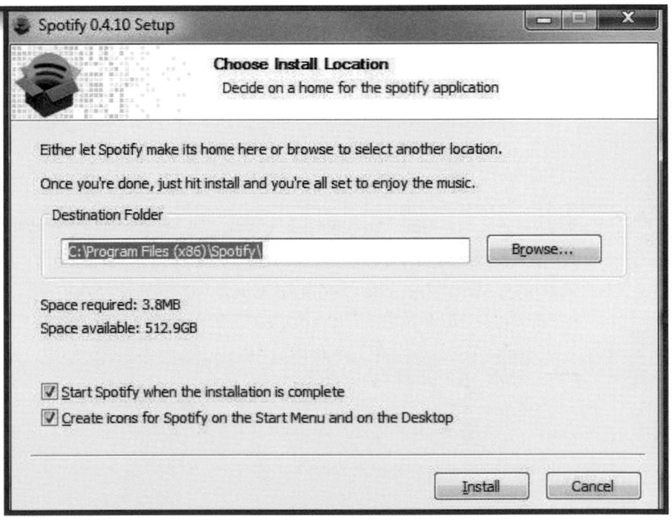

Spotify 0.4.10 Setup

Choose Install Location
Decide on a home for the spotify application

Either let Spotify make its home here or browse to select another location.

Once you're done, just hit install and you're all set to enjoy the music.

Destination Folder

C:\Program Files (x86)\Spotify\   Browse...

Space required: 3.8MB
Space available: 512.9GB

☑ Start Spotify when the installation is complete
☑ Create icons for Spotify on the Start Menu and on the Desktop

Install   Cancel

8

Spotify should now start. Enter your user name and password (from Step 2) and click Sign In. You can check the 'remember me' box to save having to sign in again next time.

Spotify

Spotify™

Username
angusfridge

Password
****

Forgot your password?

☐ Remember me   Sign in

9 To get started, enter the name of any artist or song in the search box and enjoy the music.

10 Somewhat unusually, when you click the close button in Spotify, the program does not actually close completely. Rather, it minimises to the Taskbar. To close it completely, right click the Taskbar icon and select Exit.

11 To open Spotify again, look for it in the Start menu or type Spotify in the search panel just above the Start button.

Uninstalling a program

There will come a time when you no longer have a need for one or more of your programs. Once uninstalled, a program can no longer be run on your computer. You can always *reinstall* it, of course, providing you still have the original disc or download file.

One point to note: uninstalling a program does not usually remove any files that you created yourself with it. Uninstalling Word, for instance, does not delete your letter files. However, because programs often use proprietary file formats, you may find that you can no longer access your files without the original program. The moral of which is: take care and use non-proprietary file formats wherever possible.

❶

Start

Control Panel

Uninstall a program

We're back in the Control Panel now. The uninstall feature is in the Programs section.

❷

[Program]

Uninstall

All you have to do is find the program you wish to uninstall – in this case, Spotify – and click it once to select it. Then click the Uninstall button in the menu bar near the top of the window. Follow any prompts on screen and that's it.

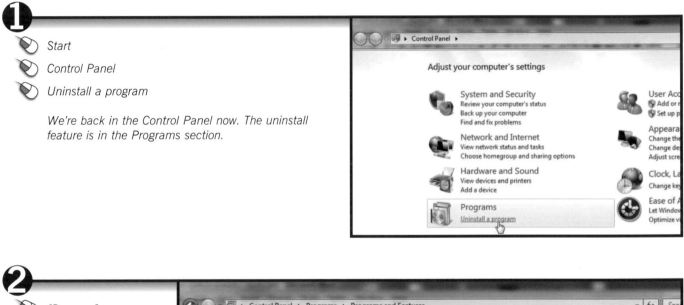

Unfreezing your computer

Windows is designed for multi-tasking i.e. for doing several things at once. This means that you can easily run two, three or more programs at the same time – perhaps an e-mail program, a web browser, a word processor and a music player.

However, there are certain limitations. Without getting too technical, the number of programs and tasks you can perform simultaneously depends on how much memory your computer has and, to a lesser extent, the speed of its processor. If you try to do too much, everything will slow to a crawl and you'll spend more time drumming your fingers on your desk waiting for windows to open than typing on your keyboard. In the worst case, your computer may actually 'freeze'. No matter what you click, nothing happens: the screen display refuses to change and your computer is effectively lifeless. What to do?

Well, you have two options. First, right click any clear spot on the Taskbar and select Start Task Manager from the popup menu.

Task Manager has several tabs but you're interested in Applications. Here you'll see a list of all programs currently running on your computer. If any program is marked as 'Not Responding' in the Status, that's your culprit right there. Select the program and click End Task. Windows will now close this – *and only this* – program, and you should be able to use your computer as normal again. The downside is that any open file within that program will also close, and so you'll lose the changes you made since the last time you saved it. We'll come to that in the very next section.

If Task Manager can't resolve your troubles and your computer is absolutely frozen, there is another option – but this one is strictly for Emergency Use Only. Press the reset button on the system unit. This bypasses the usual shutdown procedure and immediately turns your computer off and on again. Here, too, you'll lose any unsaved files, and this time it affects *all* open programs. Windows may also launch a ***diagnostic utility*** before it restarts.

There's no need to panic if a program freezes your computer – Task Manager can usually save the day.

The reset button really is the last resort.

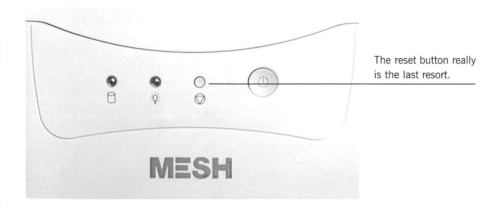

Save your work-in-progress with a button, a menu command or a keyboard shortcut.

The all-important Save button

If there's one lesson that all computer owners learn the hard way, it is this: losing your work is a nightmare. Be it a power failure, a system freeze or an accidental click on the wrong button, there's nothing like watching a critical file or project disappear forever to make you wish you'd never set eyes on your hardware.

But it needn't be so! Barring the most extreme misadventure, any file saved to your hard disk is safe. Back on page 77, we looked at how to save a new file using the Save As command. This same procedure applies in virtually all programs: you give each new file a name and save it. However, the critical thing – the really, *really* critical thing – is remembering to save your work *as you go along*.

When you first save a file, it is allocated a slice of hard disk space. However, the moment you open and change that file in any way – add or delete a word or a sentence or an image, or change the formatting, or do anything whatsoever – the open file and the saved file are no longer identical. The open file is held in a kind of flux while you work, and is vulnerable to all sorts of mishap. This is why it is vital to save your work continually. The idea is simply to minimise the period between your last save and the moment catastrophe strikes – and, since you never know when catastrophe is going to strike, this means saving your work *frequently*. We would suggest that once every couple of minutes is a good target.

How do you save your work? In almost every case, you will find a Save button on your program's Toolbar (it often looks like a floppy disk). Failing this, click File on the Menu Bar and look for the Save command.

There are some exceptions, however. E-mail programs, for instance, automatically save incoming messages without the need for you to do anything.

Alternatively, many programs allow you to use a keyboard shortcut: pressing the Ctrl + S keys simultaneously has the same effect as clicking Save.

Every time you save a file, the file on your hard disk is overwritten with the open version. If you wish to avoid this, use the Save As command instead, and save the open file with a new name. Thus you might open your 'Letter to the bank manager requesting a loan' and save it immediately as, say, 'Loan agreement details'. Now you can use the original file as a useful template without in any way affecting it.

QUICK Q & A

Shouldn't I always use non-proprietary file formats?
You may not have a choice – some programs only let you save a project with one particular file extension. Also, using a proprietary format often means that you can use special effects that just aren't possible otherwise. A document designed with bullet points, fancy fonts, text effects and so forth in Word will lose most of its formatting if saved as a plain text (.txt) file. But yes, as a rule, use a non-proprietary format when you intend to share files with others and you don't know for sure that they have the same software as you.

What does what?

The range of programs is truly vast, from free utilities to super-expensive video editing suites. Moreover, while you probably know a few of the big software names, like Microsoft, there is tremendous competition in most markets. We would strongly advise that you research any potential purchase thoroughly, as no two programs are ever quite identical. What might appear to be a minor weakness in one slightly cheaper program may, in fact, make it wholly unsuitable for your intentions; on the other hand, you can often save a good deal of money by opting for software that has a lower specification but still does all you need of it.

There is also a tremendous degree of cross-over among genres. A word processor, for instance, is perfect for writing letters (and computer manuals) but can also handle figures and even basic design and illustrative work. Don't splash out on new software if your existing programs can handle your needs.

Each new program involves another learning curve. However, Windows encourages a roughly standard interface, or appearance, so it's often possible to work out the basics fairly quickly.

These screens show very different types of program – one is designed for editing text; the other for editing images – but note the similarities. Both have a Title Bar, a Menu Bar, a number of Toolbars and a large central working area. In short, you click things – buttons, menus, icons – to make stuff happen.

QUICK Q & A

When a program asks me if I want to read the ReadMe file, what does it mean?
A ReadMe file is a text document on a program's installation disc that contains important or late-breaking news concerning the program. For instance, if a bug has been discovered since the CD-ROM was pressed, or if there is a misprint in the manual, you may find details in the ReadMe file. It might also provide help and instructions with the program installation. So, yes – always read the ReadMe.

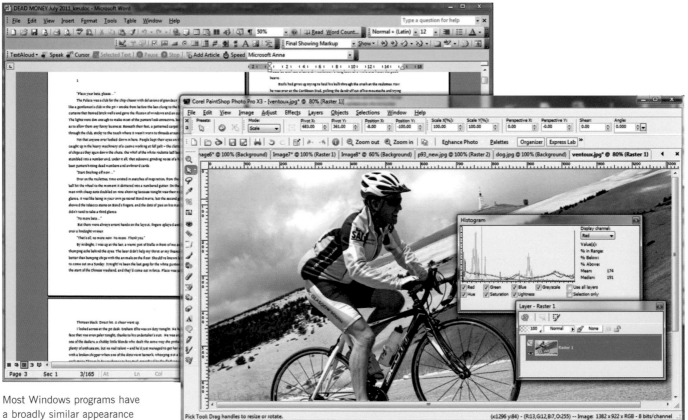

Most Windows programs have a broadly similar appearance regardless of what they actually do.

Here is a very rough, ready and by no means exhaustive
guide to popular types of program and what they do
best:

Program type	What can you do with it?
Antivirus	Prevent potentially harmful viruses from damaging your computer.
CAD (Computer Aided Design)	Design products digitally on a computer.
CD burning	Record audio, video and data compilations onto CDs.
Database	Collate and manage complex and/or large quantities of data.
DTP (Desktop Publishing)	Design documents and projects using text and images.
E-mail	Send, receive and manage e-mail messages.
Financial management	Keep tabs on your incomings and outgoings.
Firewall	Protect your computer from internet *hackers*.
Games	Play games ranging from child-friendly educational tools to blood-thirsty shoot-'em-ups.
Image editor	Edit and enhance digital pictures imported from a scanner or a digital camera.
Instant messenger	Exchange text messages across the internet in real time.
Multimedia player	Play music and videos on your computer.
Office suite	Use a compendium of business tools, typically including a word processor, spreadsheet, database, e-mail and PIM.
PIM (Personal Information Manager)	Keep track of your contacts with an address book, diary and calendar.
Presentation	Create professional presentations, particularly suited to sales proposals.
Project management	Control a complex project from conception to completion.
Reference	Carry out general and specific research – dictionary, encyclopaedia, atlas, etc.
Sound editor	Record and edit digital sound files, including musical instruments.
Speech recognition	Train your computer to recognise your voice (well, up to a point).
Spreadsheet	Perform advanced calculations with figures laid out in rows and columns.
System utilities	Maintain and trouble-shoot your computer at a sub-Windows level.
Video editor	Turn raw camcorder footage into a polished movie.
Web browser	Visit web pages and sites on the internet.
Web editor	Design and build your own web pages.
Word processor	Create and edit text-based documents.

PART 4 The internet

For many of us, connecting to the internet is the single most useful thing we can do with our PC. It gives us access to e-mail, instant messaging and social networks, such as Facebook; it delivers breaking news, encyclopaedic knowledge and expert advice; it delivers voice and video chat, music streaming and video downloads; and it provides online shopping, deep discounts and really useful product advice. All this and much, much more is available at the click of a mouse.

In this section, we discover everything you need to know about the internet: how to get connected, how to visit web pages, how to find what you're looking for and how to download things to your computer. We'll also discover the simple steps that keep you safe when you're connected.

PART 4 **Getting online**

Getting onto the internet couldn't be simpler: all you need is a PC, a phone line (or mobile phone coverage) and an account with an Internet Service Provider (ISP, for short).

ISPs offer three kinds of internet access: dial-up connections, broadband and mobile broadband. Of the three, dial-up is almost obsolete; in the space of a few short years, it's gone from ubiquity to obscurity. In the 1990s, it was the only way the average person could get online; now, it's only really used where broadband and mobile broadband aren't available. That's good news, because dial-up connections are desperately slow. To do anything useful online today, you really need a broadband internet connection. Even something as simple as *online shopping* can be a real chore without it, as today's websites are largely designed for broadband-connected users.

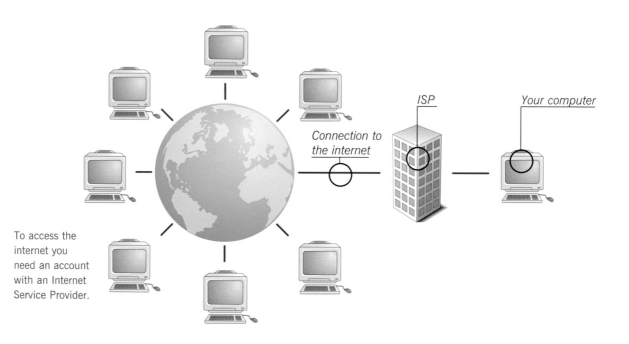

To access the internet you need an account with an Internet Service Provider.

Broadband explained

Broadband isn't a single technology. It's a catch-all term for super-fast internet connections. In the UK, they come in one of two flavours: ADSL (Asynchronous Digital Subscriber Line) or cable. ADSL comes via a standard phone line and cable broadband comes via the same cables used to deliver cable TV. If you're wondering what 'asynchronous' means in this particular case, it means that the upload and download speeds are different: a typical ADSL connection downloads files between two and 20 times more quickly than it can upload files.

As the name suggests, mobile broadband is broadband that's delivered via the mobile phone network. It's not quite as fast as normal broadband but it works anywhere you can get a 3G mobile data connection. This means most of the UK population, although coverage can be patchy in rural areas. Coverage and speeds will improve over the next few years as mobile phone companies invest in so-called 4G (fourth generation) technology but, even now, mobile broadband offers a reasonable combination of performance and mobility.

So how do you actually connect to these services? With *dial-up*, everything you need is almost certainly built into your PC. Most PCs have a *modem* port, which you connect to your phone line, and you use Windows' integrated dialler to connect to your ISP. It's worth mentioning that doing this means you can't use your phone until you disconnect and you may incur expensive per-minute call charges while you're online. We'd strongly advise against using dial-up unless you're in a rural area where broadband and mobile broadband can't reach you.

With broadband, you'll need a special broadband modem. In many cases this modem is built into a device called a router, which enables you to connect several devices to the same connection. Many routers can also be used to create a wireless network, so you can connect to your broadband service from anywhere in the house. Broadband modems and routers come in two forms, *ADSL* and *cable*. An ADSL modem or router won't work on a cable connection and vice versa.

For mobile broadband, you'll need an integrated modem, a data card or a dongle. A mobile data card is an add-on card that slots into a compatible laptop. The card contains a mobile broadband modem that connects the computer to the mobile phone network. A dongle is the same thing, but it plugs into a spare USB port rather than into a card slot – which is useful, as most computers don't come with card slots suitable for mobile data cards.

Some laptops are sold with an integrated modem, which is effectively a data card that has been built into the computer. Small 'netbook' laptops are where you'll usually find integrated modems and they're often sold by the mobile phone companies themselves. This is usually on a contract basis, so instead of buying the computer up-front you get it free or cheap on a 12-, 18- or 24-month contract.

There is another kind of mobile broadband: Wi-Fi, which is the name we use to describe wireless networks. Many public places, such as hotels, railway stations, pubs and hotels provide wireless connections, and you can use those connections to get online if your computer has a Wi-Fi modem installed. Almost every laptop on the market today includes built-in Wi-Fi. It's a great way of getting online during trips to cities but, for most of us, it isn't an alternative to fixed or mobile broadband. Wi-Fi access points become very thin on the ground when you move away from city centres.

Choosing a broadband service

For normal broadband, the choice of ADSL versus cable is often made for you: cable broadband is only available in cabled areas, which usually means areas covered by Virgin Media. If you're in an area where both kinds of connection are available, you'll often find that the cable service is faster. That's because, in most of the UK, phone connections use copper wiring; cable uses speedier fibre-optic cabling.

When you're choosing a broadband service, there are four things to consider: price is important, of course, but it's not the only factor. You also need to consider the speed of the connection, whether it's limited in any way and whether you want the ISP to provide the hardware or if you'll take care of that yourself.

What do the speeds mean?

Broadband speeds are measured in megabits per second (Mbps) and tend to be advertised as 'up to' – so, for example, an ISP might advertise their service as having a speed 'up to 8Mbps'. That sounds great but, unfortunately, the reality falls somewhere short. In 2011, telecoms watchdog Ofcom found that the average UK broadband speed was less than half the 'up to' speed quoted.

Are we being stuffed? Not really, although ISPs' adverts could certainly be more honest. The problem is that with ADSL, speeds are dependent on distance. If your house is right on top of the telephone exchange, you'll get something close to the speed promised in the adverts; if you're 1km from the exchange, you won't. And unfortunately, most of us don't have houses right on top of a telephone exchange.

Distance is less of an issue with fibre-optic connections. Virgin Media's cable services and BT's fibre-optic Infinity service deliver what they promise to deliver.

So what should you look for? As a rule of thumb, if you're considering ADSL then cut the advertised speed in half – so if it's advertised as 'up to 8Mpbs', expect 4Mbps. Anything over 1Mbps is fine for everyday use, but if you want to watch high-definition video, such as HD programmes from the BBC's iPlayer or Channel 4's 4oD, then you'll need at least 2Mbps of real-world speed, ideally more. Unless you're planning to do a lot of downloading, there's no real reason to pay extra for the speediest broadband connections.

It's worth mentioning Wi-Fi again here. If you're planning to use Wi-Fi with your broadband, make sure your wireless kit is up to the job: if you connect to a 50Mbps broadband service with an 802.11b wireless network adapter, you're throwing your money away. 802.11b kit has a theoretical maximum speed of 11Mpbs and a real-world speed of around 5Mbps – so you'd be paying for a broadband connection that's ten times faster than your hardware can handle!

Fibre-optic services, such as Virgin Media's cable broadband and BT's Infinity broadband, deliver the speeds they promise. ADSL speeds depend on distance.

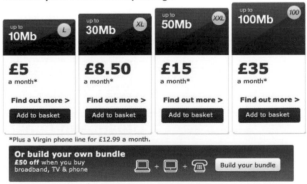

Choose your broadband package

*Plus a Virgin phone line for £12.99 a month.

Mobile broadband dongles plug into your laptop's USB port and connect you to the mobile phone data network.

What about mobile speeds?

Mobile broadband speeds are even more unpredictable than normal broadband. The speed you get depends on the strength of the signal, how far away you are from the cell towers, how many other people are trying to connect at the same time and myriad other factors. Take the phone firms' adverts with a hefty pinch of salt. In 2011, the Top10 comparison website tested thousands of connections and found that, despite advertised speeds of up to 7Mbps or more, average mobile speeds were between 2Mbps and 3Mbps, with many users struggling to get even that.

To cap or not to cap?

Many ISPs use a combination of capping and traffic management technology to limit what customers can do. Caps are a straightforward usage limit; for example, the cheapest broadband services may give you a 'fair use limit' of 1GB per month. If you download more data than that, your connection may be slowed down or stopped, or you may have to pay extra. 1GB is fine for occasional use – a few hours per week browsing the web and sending and receiving e-mails – but it's useless for services such as *streaming* online video, which will hit the limit in a matter of hours.

Traffic management could have an effect too. ISPs can prioritise some kinds of data over others so, for example, they might slow down file downloads and prioritise voice chat so that people's calls don't suffer. Not every ISP uses such technology, but at the time of writing the ISPs' organisation, the Broadband Stakeholder Group (BSG), is preparing a code of conduct where every ISP will be open about what, if any, traffic management they use – so if they slow down services such as iPlayer, they'll tell you about it.

The combination of 'up to' speeds, caps and traffic management means it's important to shop around. If you can get online, sites such as ISP Review (**www.ispreview.co.uk**), Broadband Genie (**www.broadbandgenie.co.uk**) and Money Supermarket (**www.moneysupermarket.com/broadband**) can help guide you through the maze of available services – not just for fixed broadband, but for mobile too.

Broadband bundles

As if broadband wasn't confusing enough, many operators now offer bundles: for a single monthly fee you get not just broadband, but other services too: free phone calls, perhaps, or a TV service, or free access to Wi-Fi connections when you're

Many ISPs offer bundles, where you pay once and get broadband, telephone services and sometimes TV services too.

out and about. In some cases, the broadband is the free bit; for example, at the time of writing, Sky offers a Sky TV bundle with free calls and broadband for £19.50 a month.

Are bundles worth the money? Inevitably, there are pros and cons. The right bundle can be more cost-effective than having separate phone, broadband and TV services and having a single monthly bill is certainly easier. Then again, some bundles offer very basic, capped broadband that isn't appropriate for heavy internet use. The answer, then, really depends on what particular services you want to use.

Who supplies the hardware?

Almost every ISP will happily provide you with the necessary hardware to get your PC online, usually in the form of a combined modem/router that enables you to connect PCs wirelessly to your broadband connection. There are two things to think about here: what the router does and how much the ISP charges for it.

There are several flavours of Wi-Fi: 802.11a, 802.11b, 802.11g and 802.11n. Of the four, the newest 802.11n technology is the fastest and the least prone to interference. We wouldn't attempt to watch high-definition video on the internet with anything slower. If your ISP isn't providing an 802.11n-compatible router, it might be a good idea to buy one yourself. Make sure you buy the right kind, though: an ADSL model for ADSL connections or a cable one for cable connections.

Increasingly, ISPs offer wireless modems/routers for free. Not all ISPs do, though, and it's a good idea to use a price-checking service such as Kelkoo (**www.kelkoo.co.uk**) to see if you can get a router for less than the ISP charges. You often can.

Don't forget that you can't connect to a wireless network if your PC doesn't have a wireless network adapter. If you've bought a laptop in the last few years, it almost certainly has a wireless adapter in it, but desktop PCs are rarely wireless-enabled. The good news is that you can buy USB wireless adapters for around £10 if you shop around. Make sure the adapter is the same standard as the router, so if the router is 802.11n then buy an adapter that also supports 802.11n Wi-Fi. Other Wi-Fi adapters will work but they'll be significantly slower.

Once you've chosen your ISP and organised your router or modem, it's time to connect. The process is very simple and doesn't take long. Let's get connected!

If you're buying a wireless router, go for the fastest 802.11n standard. It doesn't cost much more than other kit and you'll regret it if you buy something slower.

Connecting to broadband

To connect to broadband, you'll need one of two things: a USB modem (or dongle, if it's for mobile broadband) or a modem/router. USB devices are simple to install: simply plug them into a spare USB port and run the installer from the supplied CD or DVD. When prompted, enter the username and password your ISP or mobile phone provider gave you. Connecting a router takes a little more effort, but not much more.

In this section, we discover how to connect a router and set up a wireless network. If you're using a USB modem and don't intend to share your broadband with any other devices over Wi-Fi, please skip this section and go straight to 'Browsing the web' (page 110).

The first step is to connect the broadband cable, which looks like a telephone cable, to the back of the router. If you're using ADSL broadband, connect the other end to a microfilter – a box that splits your phone line into two connections, one for the phone and the other for the broadband – which plugs into the phone socket. If your ISP provided you with a router, it should have supplied the microfilters too: without a microfilter you'll lose your internet connection whenever you use the phone. You need to put a microfilter on every phone point where you use a telephone.

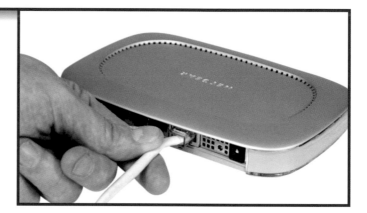

Now, you can connect your PC. We've already connected an Ethernet cable to the back of the PC, and it's just a matter of plugging the other end of the cable into one of the empty Ethernet ports on the back of the router.

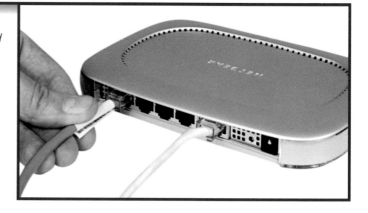

If you'll be sharing your broadband connection with more than one computer, you can do it with an Ethernet cable (as shown here): simply get a second cable, plug one end into the PC and plug the other end into the next available Ethernet port on the router. If you've got a wireless router and will be connecting your other devices via wireless, you can skip this step.

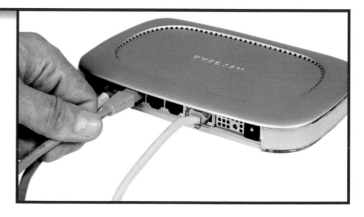

Configuring your router for broadband

Once you've set up and connected your router, the next step is to apply the appropriate settings for your broadband account. After that, we'll set up the router's wireless features. As we'll discover, it's all very straightforward.

Turn on the router, switch on your PC and launch your web browser. A router has a control panel that you access using your web browser. To use it, you need to know where it is. The default address of a Netgear router, which we're using here, is 192.168.0.1. Other manufacturers use different addresses – the number you need will be with the router's manual or the instructions from your ISP. Enter the appropriate address and then press the Enter key.

Your router is password protected to stop other people using it and changing its settings. Netgear's default settings are a username of 'admin' and a password of 'password'. You can change these from the control panel later. For now, enter the username and password and click on OK.

*Our router's various options are listed in the blue panel on the left hand side of the screen. We're looking for Basic Details; other routers may use different labels but the process is the same. You'll now be asked to provide information that you should have received from your ISP. You'll be asked to provide details of **domain** name **servers** and IP addresses here. Unless your ISP has told you otherwise, the best option here is 'get automatically from ISP'. Don't worry about the various acronyms – DNS, NAT and so on. All you need to do is ensure that the information you enter matches the information your ISP gave you.*

Once you've entered the details, your router may offer a Test button to check that everything's okay. Click on it and the router will open a new window (your browser may try to block it – if it does, you'll see a message at the bottom of the window that enables you to undo the block and see the page). What's supposed to happen next is that your browser connects to the manufacturer's website and displays a 'congratulations!' message; what's happened here is that the manufacturer has moved the page, so we get a 'Page Not Found' message instead. That's not a problem, though, because we've still loaded a web page: our broadband is working properly. We're up and running!

Cutting the cables

The combination of broadband and wireless networking is wonderful. You can get connected from anywhere in the house, using any wireless-enabled device. Shopping from the sofa, reading recipes in the kitchen, catching up on the news in the garden ... all of this is possible without running cables around the place, drilling holes in walls or expending any effort whatsoever. For best results, however, it helps to know a little bit about wireless standards.

Wireless standards

Wi-Fi is a catch-all term for various kinds of wireless network and there are four main standards: 802.11a, 802.11b, 802.11g and 802.11n. For home-networking equipment, you'll usually find three of those four standards: b, g and n. So what does that actually mean?

The letters indicate a particular version of Wi-Fi. Of the three, b is the oldest and slowest, while n is the newest and fastest. Hardware tends to be backwards compatible, so 802.11n kit will connect to 802.11g and 802.11b networks. You can't generally connect old 802.11b kit to new 802.11n networks, although some routers run in 'dual mode', effectively creating two networks so that 802.11b devices can still connect.

Why does any of this matter? The short answer is speed. 802.11b isn't fast enough for anything ambitious, such as streaming high-quality video, and it suffers badly from distance and interference: its top speed is a theoretical 11Mbps but 5Mbps is more likely. The further from the router you take your PC, the slower that speed becomes. By comparison, 802.11n hardware delivers real-world performance that's around ten times faster than 802.11b and it's much less prone to interference from the likes of radiators, walls and other electronic devices.

If you're buying Wi-Fi hardware, we'd strongly advise you to buy hardware that uses the 802.11n standard – especially if you're going to be using a reasonably fast broadband service. There's no point in paying for a 50Mbps cable broadband service if you're connecting to it with Wi-Fi kit that can barely reach 5Mbps.

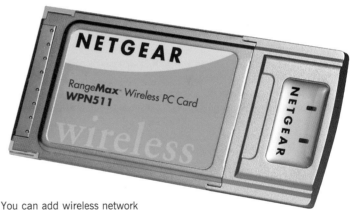

You can add wireless network support to almost any computer. Wireless adaptors come in PCI (for installing inside desktop PCs), PC card (for laptops, as shown here) or USB flavours.

Configuring a wireless network

In our last walkthrough, we showed you how to configure your router for broadband. Now, we'll use the same control panel to configure its wireless features and share the broadband connection via Wi-Fi. If you aren't still logged in to the router's control panel, please repeat steps 1 and 2 from the previous walkthrough (page 103).

This time, click on Wireless Settings in the panel at the left of the window. There are four key bits of information here: The network's name, or SSID, which can be anything you like; the region, which is usually Europe; the channel, which you can leave as is; and the mode. If your router supports more than one wireless standard, mode enables you to specify which ones it should support – so, for example, you can switch off support for 802.11b if you don't want such devices to connect. In most cases you can leave this option as is. This particular router supports b and g wireless, so the option shown here is 'g&b'. Make sure the boxes for 'enable wireless access point' and 'allow broadcast of name (SSID)' are both ticked; if they aren't, your computers won't be able to see and connect to the wireless network.

It's a very bad idea to leave your wireless network unsecured, because wireless works through walls: if you don't password protect it, what's to stop the neighbours using your connection for nefarious purposes? Under Security Options, choose WEP (Wired Equivalent Privacy) and then type a Passphrase in the 'Passphrase' box. When you click Generate, the router will create a complicated password, known as a 'key'. Take a note of this number: you'll need to enter it on any computer or device that you want to connect to your wireless network. No key, no entry!

Connecting to a wireless network

Connecting to a wireless network couldn't be simpler. If your computer has a switch that turns its wireless adapter on and off – many laptops do – make sure it's in the on position and then follow these easy steps.

1

Look for the Network icon in the bottom right of the screen – it's in the Taskbar by the clock and looks like the signal strength icon on a mobile phone. Click on the icon and you should see a list of available wireless networks. In this screenshot, we're in range of two wireless networks. That's fairly common: one of them is ours and the other one is our neighbours'.

Not connected

Connections are available

Wireless Network Connection

teh intarwebs!!!!

SKY1F320

Open Network and Sharing Center

2

Each connection has an icon showing how strong its signal is; sometimes, you'll also see an exclamation mark in a yellow shield: this means that Windows thinks there may be a problem with the connection. We've found that it sometimes appears because of a disagreement between our anti-virus software and Windows itself and it's not something you should worry about.

Not connected

Connections are available

Wireless Network Connection

teh intarwebs!!!!

Connect

SKY1F320

Open Network and Sharing Center

3

To connect to a network, click on its name and then on the Connect button that appears. If it's password protected you'll be asked for the password; if you don't know it, you won't be able to connect. A blue ring will spin over the network icon for a second or two and then you should see the 'Connected' message shown here. If you've connected to a network but it isn't then letting you access the internet, for example because the router isn't currently connected to your broadband, you'll see 'No Internet Access' in this window.

Currently connected to:

teh intarwebs!!!!
Internet access

Wireless Network Connection

teh intarwebs!!!!   Connected

SKY1F320

Open Network and Sharing Center

Connecting via dial-up

If you don't live in an area where broadband is available – or you only plan to connect to the internet from time to time, and don't fancy paying a monthly subscription – then you can still get online with a dial-up connection. Your PC probably came with a built-in modem, and as you'll see from this walkthrough it's very simple to get up and running. As with broadband, you'll need an account with an Internet Service Provider (ISP) before you can connect: in most cases they'll send you a CD that takes care of the installation for you, but some ISPs expect you to do it yourself. Here's how to do it.

Dig out the modem cable that came with your computer system. One end plugs into the 'line' socket on the modem and the other into a standard telephone socket. If there are two sockets on the modem, the second is for connecting a telephone handset, and should be clearly marked or labelled as such. Check the computer or modem manual if in doubt. Do remember that you can't use the telephone while your computer is connected to the internet. Callers will get an engaged tone.

1

 Start

 Network and Internet

 Network and Sharing Center

Once you've connected your PC to your phone line, click on the options above. You'll see a big red cross between your PC and the internet: this means you don't have a connection. Let's change that. Click on 'Set up a new connection or network'.

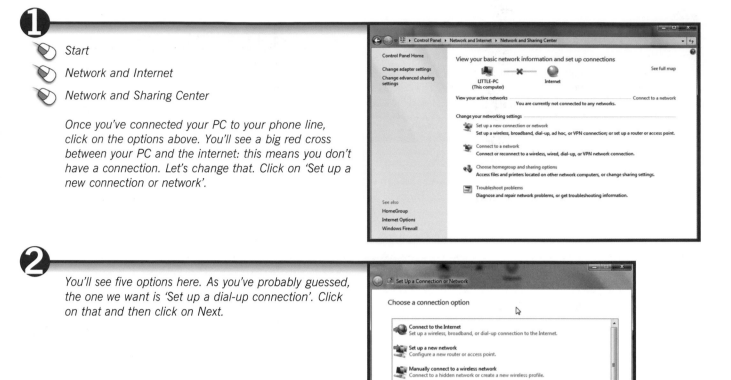

2

You'll see five options here. As you've probably guessed, the one we want is 'Set up a dial-up connection'. Click on that and then click on Next.

3

We need to enter three bits of information here: the ISP's phone number (without spaces) and the user name and password your ISP will have given you. If you want to connect automatically in future, click on 'Remember this password'. Give your connection a name and click on Connect.

4

Windows will now attempt to connect to your ISP. You may hear a series of shrieks and beeps from your PC – they're perfectly normal! The sounds you hear are simply the modem attempting to make a connection.

5

This is the screen you'll see if your modem doesn't detect a dial tone. That's usually because the modem cable isn't connected to your PC or isn't properly inserted into the phone socket. To try again, check your connections and then click Try Again. Alternatively, click on 'Set up the connection anyway' to save the details for later.

6

We've clicked on 'Set up the connection anyway' and Windows displays this screen to let you know that the details have been saved. The network icon it refers to is the one near the clock at the bottom right of your screen: it's shaped like the signal strength icon on a mobile phone.

7

Click on the network icon and you'll see a list of available connections, in this case including the dial-up connection we've just created. Windows should connect automatically whenever you try to access a web page or internet service, but you can also connect and disconnect manually by clicking on your connection in this window. Remember to disconnect when you're finished: most dial-up services incur per-minute telephone charges, which can soon mount up.

PART 4 Browsing the web

Congratulations: you've successfully set up your internet connection! Now it's time to start exploring the World Wide Web using a web browser called Internet Explorer. Once you've mastered a few straightforward features, you'll be able to find and view any website anywhere in the world.

What is a web browser?

A web browser is a computer program designed to display web pages. The best way to think of it is as a window on the World Wide Web: through it you can read interesting articles, watch videos, listen to music and even work on documents. So what do we mean by web pages and the World Wide Web – and where does the internet fit into all of this?

Imagine millions of computers all over the world, all connected to each other. That's the internet. It doesn't really do anything; it's the electronic glue that connects all those computers together. Services then use the internet to send and receive stuff. For example, e-mail software uses the internet to send and receive messages; services such as Skype use the internet to make telephone and video calls; and the bulk of the information we see online is usually transmitted via the World Wide Web.

The World Wide Web is a standard way of sharing information: the idea is that you should be able to access any web page provided you know its web address and have a web browser. It shouldn't matter whether you're on a Windows machine or an Apple one, using a smartphone or connecting from a tablet computer. What you see should be the same no matter what kind of machine you use to get online.

Inevitably it's a little bit more complicated than that – for example, many sites use an animation and video technology called Flash that doesn't work until you install a program called the Flash Player – but if you've got a recent web browser you shouldn't encounter problems accessing mainstream websites (and if you need to install additional software, your browser will tell you).

So what does the browser actually do? When you enter a web address (or click on a link on a page you're currently viewing), your browser works out where on the internet that page actually lives. It then sends a message to the computer asking for a copy of the page and its contents, which might include photos, animation, video or music. The computer sends the necessary pieces, your browser puts them all together and your PC displays the website you asked your browser to display.

There are lots of web browsers to choose from, but for this tutorial we'll stick with Microsoft's Internet Explorer. There are three reasons for that. First, it's installed automatically with every copy of Windows. Secondly, it's been designed to make browsing the internet as user-friendly as possible. And thirdly, it's really rather good.

Do you need a different browser?

While every copy of Windows comes with Internet Explorer, other browsers are available. We'd recommend sticking with Internet Explorer while you're finding your feet, but once you're up and running you might find that rival browsers are better suited to your way of doing things. At the time of writing the best alternatives to Internet Explorer are all free. We'd recommend these:

- **Google Chrome (www.google.com/chrome)** Stripped-back and straightforward, Chrome is very, very fast and works particularly well with Google services such as Google Docs.
- **Opera (www.opera.com)** Some really clever ideas and a beautiful user interface make Opera well worth checking out. It's fast, packed with handy time-saving features and a joy to use.
- **Firefox (www.mozilla.com/firefox)** A little more complex than its competitors but, if you want a browser that can do absolutely everything, this is the one to choose.

Google Chrome is an alternative, simple, free web browser. Why not give it a try?

chrome   English (UK)

Get a fast, free web browser

Google Chrome runs websites and applications with lightning speed.

Download Google Chrome

It's free and is installed in seconds

For Windows XP, Vista and 7

Fast start-up
Google Chrome launches immediately.

Fast loading
Google Chrome loads websites quickly.

Fast search
Search the internet directly from the address bar.

Learn about Google Chrome »

©2011 Google - Privacy Policy - Help - Google Chrome for Mac or Linux

Browser basics

To launch your browser, click on Start > Internet Explorer. After a second or two, you should see a screen like the one below. Let's discover what each bit does.

Forward and back buttons These buttons enable you to retrace your steps; for example, if you click on the back arrow, the browser displays the page you visited before the page you're currently viewing.

Address bar This is where you type the address of a site you'd like to visit and it's where Internet Explorer displays the address of the site you're currently seeing. You'll see some little icons to the right of this bar: the looking glass tells the browser you want to carry out a web search; the ripped page is for when you encounter an old web page that doesn't work properly – clicking on it tries to fix the problem; the circle arrow reloads the current page (and turns into a Go button with a forward-pointing arrow when you type something); and the X button stops loading a page. The X button is handy if a page is taking too long to load.

Tab Internet Explorer can handle more than one web page at a time. The tab showing 'Hotmail' is the page you're currently seeing, but if you click on the square to the right you'll get a new, blank tab that you can open a different page in. You can then switch between open pages by clicking on the appropriate tabs.

Minimize, Maximize and Close buttons These are the standard Windows buttons: Minimize reduces Internet Explorer to a button on the Taskbar; Maximize makes Internet Explorer take up the full screen; and Close closes the browser altogether. To prevent annoying accidents, if you have multiple tabs open, Internet Explorer will ask if you're sure when you click on Close.

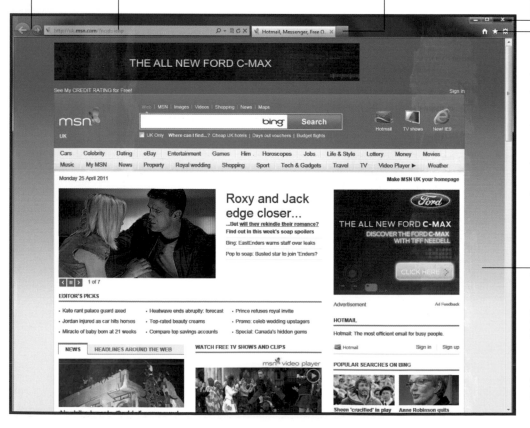

Home, Favorites and Options buttons Clicking on Home takes you to your home page – MSN if you haven't changed it – while Favorites (Microsoft's spelling, not ours!) displays the Favorites menu. More of that in a moment. The last icon, the one that looks like a cog, brings up Internet Explorer's various options.

Web page As you can see, almost all of the browser is given over to the web page you're currently visiting – in this case, Microsoft's MSN.com. By default, Internet Explorer visits MSN whenever you first open it, although you can change that setting if you like.

*Using the mouse, click in the Address Bar. This will highlight the current address – usually MSN – in blue. Now type **bbc.co.uk/news** and press the return key.*

*Ta-da! We now have the BBC news website. If you look in the Address Bar, you'll see that Internet Explorer has added some extra letters to the address, which now starts with **http://www.**. Internet Explorer does that automatically to make things simpler: in older browsers, you had to remember to do it yourself. To view a story, simply click on the headline. Each headline is a 'link' – that is, it's something you click on to see something else. The entire World Wide Web is built around links.*

*Now, click on the square immediately to the right of the tab that says 'BBC News – Home'. You should see the 'Your Most Popular sites' screen shown here, although if this is your first time using Internet Explorer it won't know what your favourite sites are. Click in the Address Bar, type **google.com** and press the return key.*

Here's Google! The BBC News page is still open and you can visit it by clicking on the BBC News tab. To return to Google, click its tab. When you're viewing Google, look in the Address bar: once again the browser has added **http://www.** to the address but, if you look closely, you'll see that instead of **google.com** we're viewing **google.co.uk**. That's because Google can tell roughly where in the world we are and it tailors its site accordingly.

Let's do a search. In the box in the centre of the Google page, type something you'd like to search for. In this example, we'll search for Haynes Publishing. Google automatically displays the results it thinks best match our search criteria.

Don't click on anything just yet, but see what happens when you move the mouse cursor over the title of a search result: Internet Explorer displays a small picture so you can see what the site looks like. This is an enormous time saver, because you can see at a glance whether the site is what you're looking for.

Clicking on the title of the search result will open that page in the current tab, but if you right click with your mouse you'll get some useful options: you can open the link in a new tab or in a new window, you can translate it with Bing's free translation service, you can save the target to your computer (handy if it's an image or a file of some kind) or you can e-mail the link using your e-mail program. Try clicking on 'Open in new window'.

8

Your chosen link should now appear in a new browser window. Your existing window is still there, just tucked behind the new one. This can be handy if you're researching something, so for example you might have product reviews open in one window and various online shops open in another.

In a nice touch, Windows 7 makes it easy to see what tabs and windows you have open: move your mouse over the Internet Explorer icon in the Taskbar and little previews will pop up, each one showing a miniature version of an open page. To move between them, just move the mouse over them.

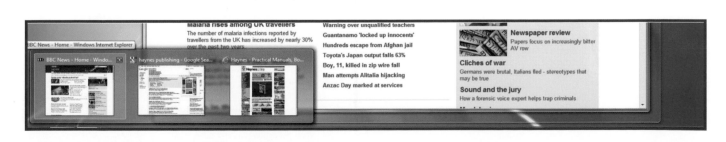

Saving favourite pages for later

With billions of pages to choose from, it's a very good idea to remember where interesting pages are so that you can find them quickly later. That's what Internet Explorer's Favorites menu is for. Let's find out how it works.

When you've found a site you'd like to save for later, click on the star icon in the top right corner of the browser window. This will display Internet Explorer's Favorites menu. To add the current page to your Favorites, click on Add To Favorites.

A pop-up window will appear. You can do several things here. In the Name field, you can change the name under which the Favorite will appear – so for example, you might change your bank's page's title from 'Login to Digital Banking' to 'Natwest' – and the Create In dropdown enables you to specify where the page should be stored.

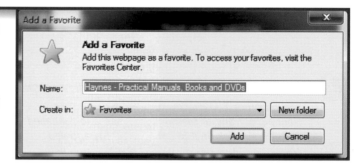

If you click on the Favorites dropdown, you'll see a list of available folders and you can store your Favorite in a particular folder by clicking on it. You can create your own folders, too, which is a very good idea: it won't be long before you have dozens of favourite websites. To create a new folder, click on New Folder.

4 The first step is to give your new folder a descriptive name. In this example, we'll go for 'Reference'. Click on the 'Create In' dropdown when you've done this. If you click on Favorites, your page will be stored in the main Favorites menu; if you select a subfolder, it'll be stored in that subfolder. The exception is the Favorites Bar, which does things slightly differently. Click on it to continue.

5 Internet Explorer will take you back to the Add a Favorite dialogue box. Click on Add to save your bookmark for later. Now, we'll display the Favorites Bar.

6 Internet Explorer hides menus and extra toolbars by default, but it's easy to bring them back. Press the Alt key and you'll see the familiar File, Edit and View menus. Click on View > Toolbars > Favorites Bar to display the Favorites Bar.

7 The Favorites Bar will now appear just below the Address Bar and at the right you'll see a folder called Reference. Click on it to see its contents and you should see the page you've just saved.

Downloading files

Internet Explorer doesn't just display information: it can save images, music files, video clips, software or documents from the internet to your hard disk too. This process is called 'downloading' and it's very simple and straightforward. In this section, we'll download and install some useful software and we'll learn how to save interesting pictures we've found on the internet.

Downloading software from Microsoft

Microsoft's excellent Windows Live Essentials provides free tools for e-mail, photos, chat and even editing movies and it's well worth having. The first step is to visit **get.live.com** *and click on the Download Now button.*

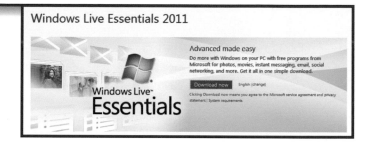

A yellow status bar will pop up at the bottom of the screen telling you how big the download is and asking whether you want to Run or Save the file. If you click Cancel here, the download won't start.

Selecting Run will download and run the file, but if something goes wrong you'll have to re-download it. For that reason, we'd recommend clicking the arrow to the right of the Save button and selecting Save and Run.

④

> Also included in Windows Live Essentials
>
> Writer   Family Safety   Mail   Messenger Companion
>
> Running security scan...   View downloads   ✕

The download will start – and if you're on a fast broadband connection, it'll finish in the time it takes you to blink. Windows will now flash up a User Account Control box asking whether you want the software to make changes to your computer. Click on Yes to continue.

⑤

You have a choice: you can install the whole Windows Live Essentials suite or you can pick and choose specific programs. Let's go for the lot. Click on Install all of Windows Live Essentials to continue.

> Windows Live Essentials 2011
>
> ## What do you want to install?
>
> Any existing Windows Live programs will be closed and updated automatically to the latest version.
>
> → **Install all of Windows Live Essentials (recommended)**
> Windows Live Essentials includes: Messenger, Photo Gallery, Movie Maker, Mail, Writer, Family Safety, Windows Live Mesh, Messenger Companion, Bing Bar, Outlook Connector Pack, and Microsoft Silverlight.
>
> → **Choose the programs you want to install**
>
> By clicking an installation option you agree to the Microsoft service agreement and privacy statement. You will get updates for this and other Microsoft programs from Microsoft Update. This software may also download and install some updates automatically.
>
> Privacy   Service agreement   Learn more

⑥

The installer will now display a progress bar as it downloads and installs the various Windows Live programs. The installer will tell you when the process is finished and you'll then be able to launch the programs from Start > All Programs > Windows Live.

> Windows Live Essentials 2011
>
> Installing Windows Live Essentials 2011
>
> ⌄ View Details   Cancel

Installing software from other firms

Microsoft makes Windows and Internet Explorer, so you'd expect its software to download and install nice and smoothly. But what about software from other firms? The good news is that the process is just as simple – but it's a little bit more annoying too.

Let's install something fun: the free WinAmp media player. To get hold of it, visit **www.winamp.com** *and click on the Free Download button.*

After a few seconds, the download should start. If it doesn't, there's a link in the page that will start the download manually. As before, Internet Explorer displays a yellow status message asking if you want to run, save or cancel the download. Use the dropdown to select Save and Run.

9 *Once the download is finished, the installer will start. After a few screens of bumph and legalese, you'll be asked where you want to install the software. The default location, Program Files, is fine. Click on Next.*

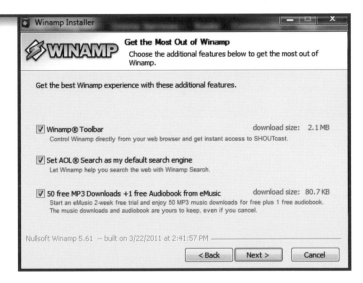

10 *This is one of our internet pet hates: software that, if you're not careful, installs a whole bunch of things you didn't ask for. If you don't untick these boxes, the WinAmp installer will add a toolbar to Internet Explorer, change your default search engine to AOL and start a two-week trial of the eMusic service. Untick the boxes and then click on Next.*

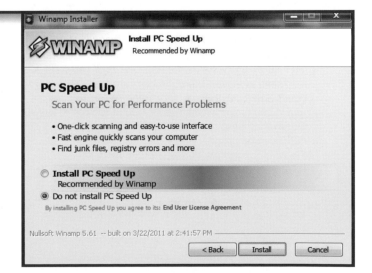

11 *WinAmp isn't finished with us yet: now it wants us to install PC Speed Up, apparently unaware of the irony that the best way to slow down a PC is to install a whole bunch of unnecessary software on it. We'd suggest clicking on Do Not Install PC Speed Up before clicking on the normal Install button.*

Downloading a photo to your PC

In addition to software, you might want to download a file from a website link – an MP3 music file, perhaps, a PDF document or an image. Here's how to do it.

The image on screen here is a link: if you click on it, it opens an even bigger version of the picture in Internet Explorer. If we right click on it, we get a range of options including 'Save picture as', 'E-mail picture' and 'Print picture'. The one we're interested in, though, is 'Save Target As…': this enables you to download the file the picture links to – in this example, that means the full-size, high-resolution photo.

Selecting 'Save Target As' brings up the familiar Windows Save As dialogue box, which enables you to change the file name and the place you're saving it to. Clicking on Save copies the file from the website and saves it on your hard disk. Remember that images on the internet may be protected by copyright: don't assume that because you've been able to download it, you're allowed to use it for anything other than looking at!

The same process works with links to other kinds of media. For example, if a web page has a link saying 'click here to download the MP3' – MP3 is a digital music file that works in software such as WinAmp, in iTunes and on iPods – then clicking on Save Target As will enable you to save the linked file to disk.

Changing the way Internet Explorer does things using the menus

Everybody is different and what suits one person might not suit another. That's why Internet Explorer can be customised to suit your particular way of working. There are two ways of doing that: via the menu bar and via the Internet Options dialogue box.

To display Internet Explorer's menu bar, press the Alt key on your keyboard. You should now see the familiar File, Edit, View and so on appear just above the web page, immediately underneath the Address Bar. Here's what the different menus offer:

View menu This is where you change what Internet Explorer displays and how it displays it. You can enable or disable toolbars, increase or decrease the text zoom and activate Full Screen mode. Full Screen mode hides everything – even the Address Bar tucks itself away at the top of the screen – so you can concentrate on the content of the current page.

Tools menu Here you'll find key features including the popup blocker, which prevents sites from opening new browser windows, and InPrivate Browsing, which doesn't record your movements when you browse the web. InPrivate Browsing is handy when you're shopping for presents for people who have access to your PC.

File menu This is where you'll find the essential operations such as opening a new tab, printing the current web page, sending a link by e-mail and so on. If a command has an associated keyboard shortcut, the menu will show it – for example, you can create a new tab by pressing Ctrl and T.

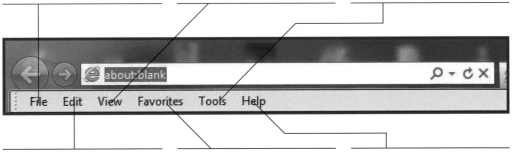

Edit menu The standard cut, copy and paste commands are in here, along with Select All and the ability to find specific text on the currently open web page.

Favorites menu This menu gives you another way to view your Favorites, add new ones or organise them into folders.

Help menu Here you can search Internet Explorer's help menu for tips, tricks and how-to information.

Changing the way Internet Explorer does things using the Internet Options dialogue box

You can change almost everything Internet Explorer does from within the Internet Options dialogue box. There are two ways to access it: click on the Tools icon (the one that looks like a cog) and then select Internet Options, or use Alt to display the menus and then select Tools > Internet Options. The dialogue box should then appear like this.

The Internet Options dialogue box is so full of features it has to be organised into tabs to keep things relatively uncluttered. Each tab covers a particular topic, as follows:

General tab This is where you can change the default home page and search engine, the colours and fonts, the way Internet Explorer handles tabs and what the browser should record when you're online.

Security tab For most of us the default security settings are fine, but if you want to make your PC more or less secure you can do that here.

Privacy tab Again, the default settings are usually fine here but, if you're feeling paranoid, you can prevent Internet Explorer from sending any information to websites and you can block cookies, which are small text files that are stored on your PC and used to tailor the adverts you see.

Content tab If you have children, this is the tab for you: here you'll find a selection of excellent *parental controls* to restrict what everyone can do and see online. You can also change the Autocomplete settings, which tell Internet Explorer what information it should automatically add to website forms.

Connections tab If you use a dial-up connection, this tab enables you to specify which connection Internet Explorer should use when it wants to get online. You can completely ignore this if you're on broadband.

Programs tab The Programs tab is where you tell Internet Explorer whether it should be the default browser – that is, the browser that runs whenever you try to view something on the internet – and what programs it should use to handle particular kinds of content. For example, you can use this section to specify which program Internet Explorer should call when you click on an 'e-mail us' link. In most cases, you don't need to change any settings here.

Advanced tab This one's for power users: in here you can control things most ordinary internet users have never heard of. Most people never need to even look at this one!

PART 4 E-mail

Away from the wonders of web pages, we find the internet's true 'killer application' – e-mail. Those of us who have been using e-mail for years now take it so much for granted that even a temporary blip in the service can induce panic ('I can't live without my Inbox!'); those who come to it anew are soon swayed by e-mail's immediacy and, dare we say it, simplicity.

Your Internet Service Provider will almost certainly provide you with an e-mail address and probably webmail access. This allows you to send and receive e-mail by logging into a web page. However, on the following pages, we're going to show you how to use one of the best e-mail services around – Gmail from Google. If you're new to e-mail, we highly recommend that you use Gmail as your main, or only, e-mail account and forget whatever service your ISP offers. If you use Gmail, your e-mail will never disappear, file sizes are less of a restriction and you can access your e-mail on any computer (or mobile phone) where you have an internet connection.

Get going with Gmail

Of the scores of *web-based e-mail* platforms available to choose from, Google's Gmail has for some time stood out from the crowd. From its clean and friendly user interface to its huge storage and revolutionary approach to organisation, it's an obvious choice.

To anyone who has spent any time on Google, the look of Gmail is familiar: a white background with little distraction and unobtrusive advertising. It also takes advantage of Google's impressive search capability when searching your Inbox. We'll talk more about that later. For now, let's get down to the nitty gritty.

*As with everything in Gmail, the sign up process is incredibly simple. Begin by typing **www.gmail.com** into your browser's address bar and click Create an account at the bottom right.*

New to Gmail? It's free and easy.

Create an account »

About Gmail   New features!

Create an Account

Your Google Account gives you access to Gmail and other Google services. If you already have a Google Account, you can sign in here.

Get started with Gmail

First name:	Josh
Last name:	Stevenson
Desired Login Name:	josh.stevenson	@gmail.com

Examples: JSmith, John.Smith

check availability!

Gmail only asks for a bare minimum of information when signing up. First off is your name. This is what appears in your friends' Inbox when you send them an e-mail. Next is your Desired Login Name. This will be the first half of your e-mail address so make it something personal. A good starting point is your name with a period between your forename and surname e.g. josh.stevenson@gmail.com. Now click the Check availability button.

Get started with Gmail

First name:	Josh
Last name:	Stevenson
Desired Login Name:	josh.stevenson	@gmail.com

Examples: JSmith, John.Smith

check availability!

josh.stevenson is not available, but the following usernames are:

- ○ stevenson.josh749
- ○ josh.joshstevenson.stevenson
- ○ jshstevenson256
- ○ stevenson.joshstevenson.josh2

Unfortunately, unless your name is extremely uncommon, there is a strong chance that it has already been taken. If so, Gmail will suggest alternatives. You can select one of these or try your own permutations and keep checking availability. A popular choice is to use the year you were born in your e-mail address e.g. josh.stevenson1979.

4

| Desired Login Name: | josh.stevenson1979 | @gmail.com |

Examples: JSmith, John.Smith

check availability!

josh.stevenson1979 is available

| Choose a password: | •••••••• | Password strength: | Good |

Minimum of 8 characters in length.

| Re-enter password: | •••••••• |

☑ Stay signed in

☑ Enable Web History Learn More

The next step is choosing your password. It is important to make your password memorable without making it easy for somebody to guess. Don't use your pet's or child's name. Gmail requires that your password has a minimum of eight characters, which may include upper case, numbers and punctuation. A combination of all three is ideal. Try switching A for 4 or S for 5. Only proceed when Gmail confirms that your password strength is at least 'good'.

| Security question: | What is the name of your best friend from childhood? ▾ |

If you forget your password we will ask for the answer to your security question. Learn More

| Answer: | Iain Smith |
| Recovery email: | kyle@scunnered.com |

This address is used to authenticate your account should you ever encounter problems or forget your password. If you do not have another email address, you may leave this field blank. Learn More

The final security factor is setting your security question. This is used in the event that you forget your password. Choose your preferred question from the dropdown menu and enter your answer in the field below. Be cautious of upper/lower case and don't get too fancy. What you type now may have to be easily remembered in two or three years' time.

Recovery e-mail is where you can enter another e-mail address to which a password reminder can be sent. If you don't have another e-mail address, ask one of your friends or family for permission to use theirs.

6

Word verification is a procedure used to prevent automated web robots from setting up Gmail accounts. Just enter the word as you see it, taking care to use proper case and punctuation if there is any. This can be surprisingly tricky! Now all that's left to do is read Google's Terms of Service and click Create my account. Congratulations, you are now the proud owner of a shiny new Gmail account.

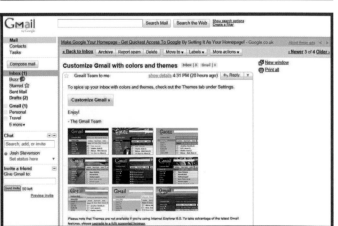

7

Gmail has its own guide to using the service but we suggest you stick with us! Click Show me my account to go straight to your e-mail Inbox.

8

Let's begin by discussing what we see on the page. At the top right, you'll see your e-mail address, along with links to Settings, Help and Sign Out. Below this near the centre you will find a search box which can be used to search your e-mail or the web. Right in the middle is your Inbox. You will already have received a few e-mails from Gmail itself.

9

Click on one of the messages from Gmail and you will see the e-mail open in the main window. This is how you read incoming messages.

Let's send an e-mail. It's an entirely painless process. Click the Compose Mail link on the left of the page. In the To field, enter somebody's e-mail address. You can send an e-mail to yourself if you like but it is better to contact a friend or family member. Enter a short subject in the Subject field (if you're e-mailing about plans for Saturday afternoon, just type Saturday Afternoon or something similar). Now write your message in the large field at the bottom. When you're finished, click the Send button, just above the To field.

If you want to send an e-mail to more than one person, you can enter multiple e-mail addresses in the To field or use the Cc (carbon copy) feature. When you Cc somebody, you are indicating that the e-mail is for their information only. If you expect a response, use the To field.

It's easy to reply to an e-mail. Here we have a new message in the Inbox. Unread messages are shown emboldened. Click on the subject line (Hi Josh, in this example) to open the message.

Now click the Reply button on the right. Because you are replying to a message, you don't have to enter a recipient's e-mail address. Your reply will go to whoever sent you the e-mail.

14 Type your reply. Your words will appear above the original message. When you're ready, click the Send button top left. Your e-mail will be sent immediately to your recipient.

↩ Reply → Forward 💬 Invite Kyle MacRae to chat

| Send | Save Now | Discard |

To: Kyle MacRae <kmacrae@gmail.com>

Add Cc | Add Bcc | Edit Subject 📎 Attach a file

B *I* U 𝓕· 𝕋· 𝕋ₐ 𝕋ₓ ⊙ 🔗 ≔ ≔ ⫤ ⫣ 66 ▤ ▤   Check Spelling ▾
▤ 𝕋ₓ « Plain Text

Yes, I would love a coffee. See you in Starbucks at 2pm|

On Mon, Apr 25, 2011 at 10:47 AM, Kyle MacRae <kmacrae@gmail.com> wrote:

Just wondering if you fancy a coffee later?

K

---

15 If you want to group e-mails from one person (or from several people with a related background, such as friends or colleagues) you can use filters and labels. When you have an e-mail open, click the little arrow next to the Reply button and select Filter messages like these.

| « Back to Inbox | Archive | Report spam | Delete | Move to ▾ | Labels ▾ | More actions ▾ |

Hi Josh Inbox | x

☆ Kyle MacRae to me   show details 10:47 AM (2 hours ago) ↩ Reply ▾

Just wondering if you fancy a coffee later?

K

	🔄 Reply to all
	→ Forward
	Filter messages like this
	Print
	Delete this message
	Report phishing
	Show original
	Message text garbled?
	Mark unread from here

↩ Reply → Forward 💬 Invite Kyle MacRae to chat

☆ ● Josh Stevenson to Kyle   show details 1:02 PM (0 m

Yes, I would love a coffee. See you in Starbucks at 2pm

---

16 There are lots of filter options but here we just want to group all messages from this sender. The sender's e-mail address will appear in the From field, so click Next Step.

Gmail
by Google

Create a Filter

Choose search criteria Specify the criteria you'd like to use for determining what to do with a message as it arrives. Use "T
messages would have been filtered using these criteria. Messages in Spam and Trash will not be searched.

From: kmacrae@gmail.com	Has the words:
To:	Doesn't have:
Subject:	☐ Has attachment

Show current filters   Cancel   Test Search   Next Step »

---

17 Now put a tick in the Apply the label box. Click the arrow next to Choose label and select New label.

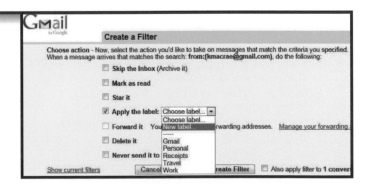

Gmail
by Google

Create a Filter

Choose action - Now, select the action you'd like to take on messages that match the criteria you specified.
When a message arrives that matches the search: from:(kmacrae@gmail.com), do the following:

☐ **Skip the Inbox (Archive it)**

☐ **Mark as read**

☐ **Star it**

☑ **Apply the label:** Choose label... ▾
    Choose label...
☐ Forward it   You New label   warding addresses.   Manage your forwarding
                    ─────
☐ Delete it   Gmail
               Personal
☐ Never send it to Receipts
               Travel
Show current filters   Cancel Work   reate Filter   ☐ Also apply filter to 1 conver

18

In the popup box, enter a name for your label (Family, in this example) and click OK.

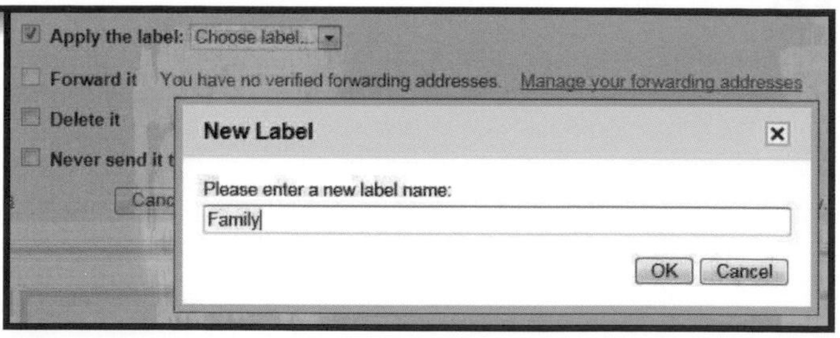

19

Now put a tick in the Also apply filter ... box and click Create Filter.

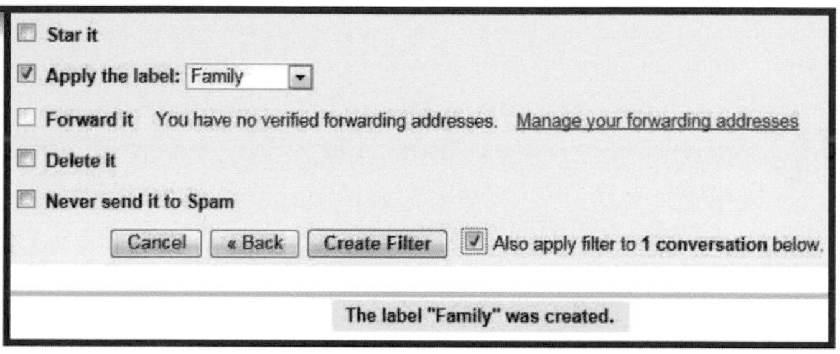

20

Back in the main Gmail window, you will find a new link on the left hand side (Family, in this example). Think of this as a folder. All new e-mails from this person will be automatically filtered into the Family link from now on. You can click Family at any time to quickly find all e-mails from this person and from any other people you filter in the same way. Create as many filters and labels as you like.

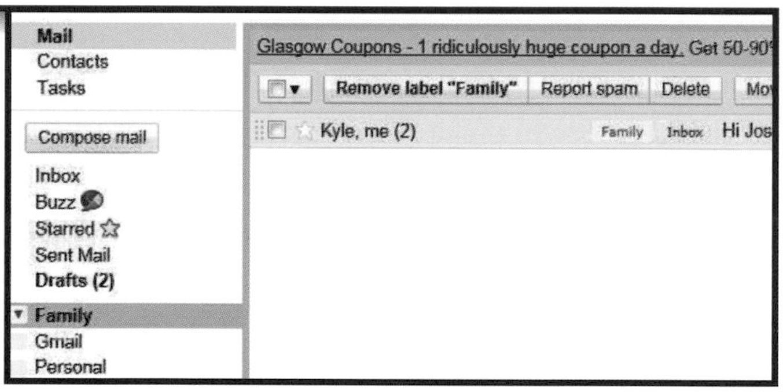

21

As you receive e-mails from people you know, you can add them as contacts in Gmail. This is very easily done. Again, click the arrow next to Reply when you're reading an e-mail in your Inbox and this time select Add to Contacts list.

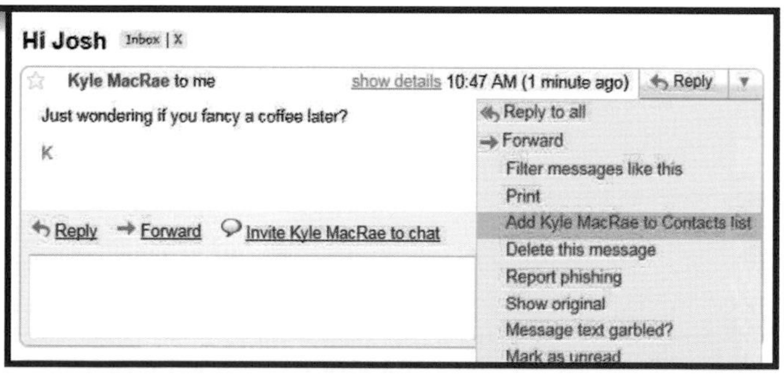

22

This done, you can find your contacts in the left column in Gmail. To send an e-mail to a contact without having to type in their e-mail address, simply put a tick in the box next to their name and click the E-mail button.

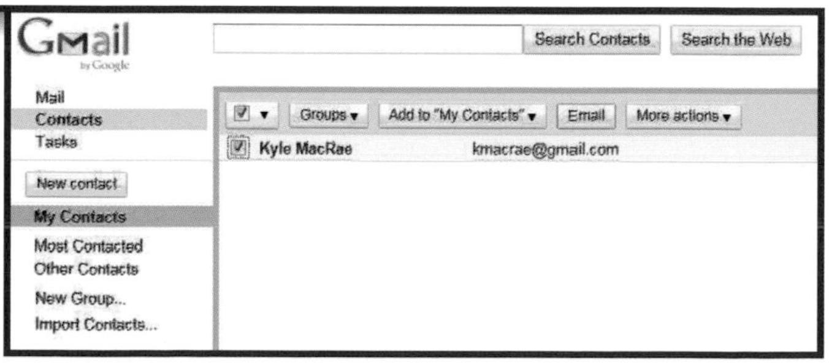

Here's a time saver. If you like to sign your e-mails in a particular way, you can create an automatic signature. Click the Settings link at the top right in Gmail and scroll down the General section until you see Signature. Click the lower radio button and enter your signature. Now click Save Changes at the bottom of the page.

Your signature will now appear at the bottom of all new e-mails that you compose and send.

Finally, there will come a time when you need to find a message you received a long time ago. If the old grey matter fails you, just enter any keyword – something from the message or the sender's name – in the search field above the Gmail Inbox and click Search Mail.

Gmail will now find all e-mails that match your search. This excellent search function is why Gmail has ignored the common method of creating folders to sort your messages (despite the fact that labels and filters are similar to folders). Whenever you need to find something, just search.

PART 4 Internet nasties

The internet is used by every kind of person you can imagine and unfortunately that means villains and other undesirables use it too. Some of them would like to infect your PC with nasty viruses, while others would like nothing better than to get their hands on your online banking password. It doesn't take much to stop them in their tracks, but doing nothing isn't an option: an unprotected PC doesn't stay unmolested for very long.

Here are the most common online irritants – and what you can do to stop them ruining your day.

Viruses and malware

Computer viruses are a huge pain in the neck and they get their name because, just like real-world viruses, they're contagious: they can spread by e-mail, by sneaking onto a USB flash drive, or across a network – and because the internet is a network, they've never been more plentiful.

The term virus is often – wrongly – used to describe all kinds of malicious code, which we should really call 'malware'. Malware could be a worm, which is a kind of program that takes advantage of unpatched security flaws to spread from machine to machine, or a Trojan horse, which pretends to be a legitimate bit of software so that it can sneak something onto your PC, or spyware, which silently monitors what you're doing and reports back to its controller. It may be designed to damage data on your hard disk, to obtain your passwords or to turn your PC into a 'bot', part of a giant network whose job is to attack websites or relay junk e-mails.

Most malware can be avoided with a few simple steps. Installing anti-malware software is a good first step – you can get decent software free from sites such as **free.grisoft.com** as well as from Microsoft. Big supermarkets' technology sections are positively stuffed with programs offering to protect your PC from every kind of online annoyance. It's also a good idea to stick to reputable websites and never open e-mail attachments you didn't expect to receive or that come from people you don't know.

Use Windows Update to keep your PC up to date and always use the most up-to-date version of your chosen web browser. Some of the most vicious and widespread malware on the internet takes advantages of security problems that browser manufacturers fixed months or even years ago, but users haven't installed the latest versions and therefore don't have the fixes. The same applies to e-mail software: use a recent program and keep it up to date. We like Windows Live Mail, which comes as part of the free Windows Live Essentials suite we downloaded earlier.

Windows comes with firewall software by default, but anti-virus and anti-spyware software isn't part of the package

– presumably because Microsoft didn't want to be accused of using its market power to crush competitors. However, Microsoft's attitude appears to have changed in recent months and the firm now offers a powerful and free security suite for Windows called Microsoft Security Essentials. To get it, visit **www.microsoft.com/en-gb/security_essentials**.

Microsoft Security Essentials is a free and powerful anti-virus and anti-spyware program that works very well with Windows 7.

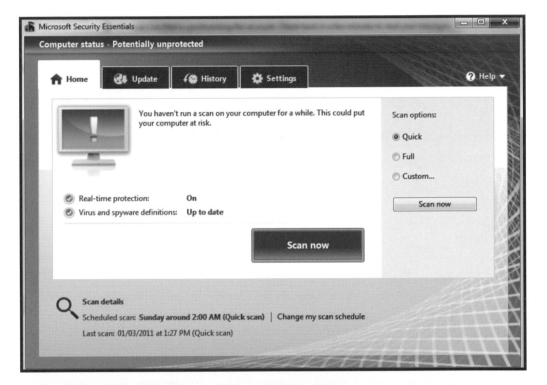

Security software needn't cost any money: the excellent AVG is free from **free.grisoft.com** and Microsoft has free security software too.

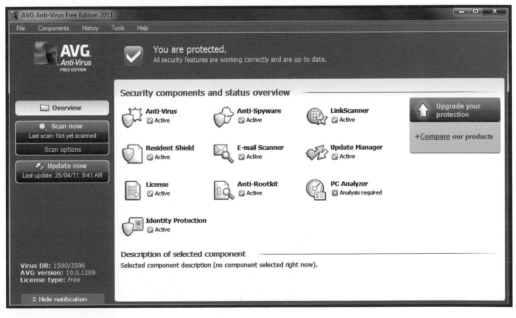

Hoaxes

'There's a secret file on your computer that spies on you for the CIA!' No, there isn't. 'There's a new and horrible virus out there and that's been confirmed by IBM and AOL today!' No, there isn't. 'Microsoft will pay you £2 for every friend you send this message to!' No, they won't.

Hoaxes don't destroy data like some malware can, but they can and do waste lots of people's time and clog up networks with rubbish. If someone sends you a virus warning – or a chain letter about some unspeakably evil everyday substance, or a hilarious letter a grandmother sent to her bank, or any other online chain letter – see if it's listed in the urban legends reference pages at **www.snopes.com**. Chances are, it's been floating about the internet for years.

Microsoft calling

It's a phone call from Microsoft: they've found a virus on your PC and they can help you fix it. Just download this special tech support software and run it. If you do, the software will confirm that your PC is riddled with unpleasantness and the 'Microsoft' person will offer to fix it in exchange for a big pile of money. They're not from Microsoft and there's nothing wrong with your PC. It's a horrible and depressingly common scam.

Phishing

This is another horrible scam. You receive an e-mail from your bank, eBay, PayPal or some other financial website. There's been a problem with your account and you need to log in to fix it. The e-mail is fake and the website it links to is fake – but, if you enter your login details, the scammers will be in your account before you can say 'international banking fraud'. Browsers such as Internet Explorer are quite good at spotting such sites if you try to load them and displaying a warning, but don't rely on your browser to tell you whether a site is legitimate or not: by the time Microsoft has spotted a fake, more fakes have been created.

Never, ever, ever, ever click on an e-mail link that appears to be from your bank, building society or any other financial firm. The messages and websites are incredibly convincing but they're still fake. If you're really worried that there might be a problem with your account, phone your local branch.

Spam, spam, spam, spam, spam

Spam – not to be confused with SPAM, which is (a) a kind of processed meat and (b) a trademark – is the everyday name for Unsolicited Commercial E-mail (UCE) or junk e-mail. It accounts for as much as 97% of all e-mails sent across the internet, for one depressing reason: it works. E-mail is so cheap that there's no difference in cost between sending to one, ten or one million people, so spam-senders don't bother refining their mailing lists. Spam is technically illegal but the likelihood of anybody being prosecuted is remote – so the junk keeps on coming.

Most of it is filtered out by our ISPs, but some still gets through. Using an e-mail program with good junk e-mail filters, such as Windows Live Mail can help, but you can also reduce the amount of spam you get by taking a few simple precautions. Never click on 'click here to unsubscribe' links or follow instructions such as 'reply to this e-mail with UNSUBSCRIBE in the header', as they just confirm that your e-mail address is live. Be careful what you opt in to when you join websites or shop online. Some shops can be sneaky, with their 'click here if you do NOT want to receive carefully selected messages' printed in text that's so small you need a microscope to read it.

It's a good idea to use multiple e-mail addresses, so for example you might have one e-mail address you give to online shops, one you use on discussion *forums* and yet another one that only your closest family, colleagues or confidants know about.

It's particularly useful to have a separate e-mail address for use with online shops because, in the UK, messages aren't junk e-mail if the sender has a commercial relationship with you – if you ordered an oven glove from a company six years ago and gave them your e-mail address, their follow-up messages aren't considered spam and the firm isn't breaking the law. Having multiple e-mail addresses is a breeze in these days of free, web-based e-mail from the likes of Hotmail and Google.

This e-mail appears to be from one of our friends, but it isn't: it's spam, sent by a computer program that's faked our friend's address and invaded his e-mail address book.

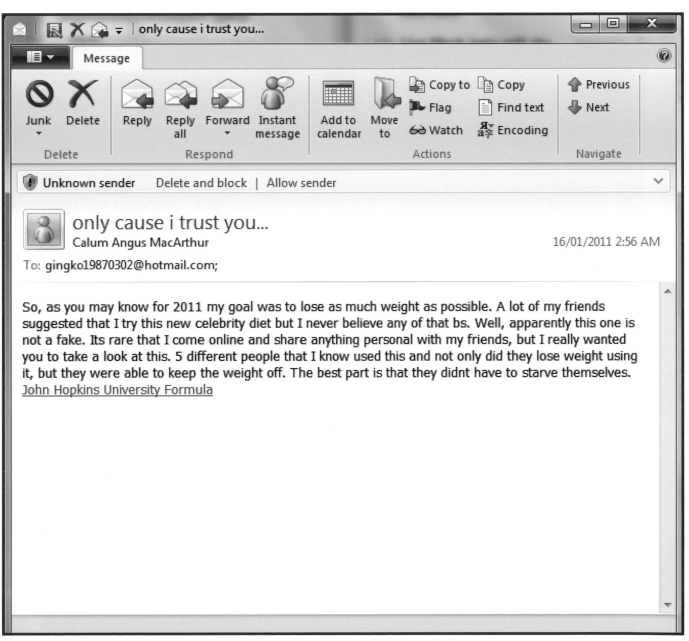

only cause i trust you...

Calum Angus MacArthur

16/01/2011 2:56 AM

To: gingko19870302@hotmail.com;

So, as you may know for 2011 my goal was to lose as much weight as possible. A lot of my friends suggested that I try this new celebrity diet but I never believe any of that bs. Well, apparently this one is not a fake. Its rare that I come online and share anything personal with my friends, but I really wanted you to take a look at this. 5 different people that I know used this and not only did they lose weight using it, but they were able to keep the weight off. The best part is that they didnt have to starve themselves.
John Hopkins University Formula

PART 5 Appendices

PART 5 Appendix 1
System Restore

On day one, your brand new computer will 'just work'. But on day two, and day three, and forever thereafter, you run the risk of trouble. One day, inevitably, your computer either won't start at all or will start misbehaving – and come that day, you'll wish that you could roll back time and undo whatever it was that caused the trouble.

Well, you can, thanks to System Restore – a rescue routine for your computer.

Good practice

System Restore works by taking regular 'snapshots' (called restore points) of your computer's most important settings. Should something go awry, you have the opportunity to revert to an earlier restore point and, hopefully, recover from the problem.

System Restore works in the background and really needs very little thought or intervention. It creates restore points automatically whenever you install a Windows Update or install a new program. However, it doesn't hurt to occasionally make restore points manually, particularly just before (not after!) making any significant change to your computer, such as plugging in a new piece of hardware. Also, because Windows doesn't *always* recognise new program installations, we'd strongly recommend that you make a manual restore point before loading any new software. Here's how …

Making and restoring a restore point

1

Start

Control Panel

System and Security

System

System Protection

System Restore

You can find System Restore by searching for it in the search box just above the Start button but this is the long way around, through the Control Panel. In the System Protection tab, click System Restore to open the tool.

2

Next

System Restore will show you the most recent restore point and invite you to select it. Click Next to proceed.

3

Finish

That's it – Windows will now restore your computer to the way it was at the selected checkpoint. Your files will remain safe and unchanged. Alternatively, ...

4

Choose a different restore point

Next

Show more restore points

If the most recent restore point doesn't fix the problem or if you suspect the problem originated with something that happened a while ago, such as a new program installation or an update, you can select the option to choose an earlier restore point in Step 2.

5

(C:)

Configure

If you want to control how and when Windows makes restore points, you can do this when you're at Step 1. Simply select your main hard drive (if you see a choice, it will always be labelled C:) and click the Configure button.

6

Here, you can turn off system restore completely – not recommended! – or increase how much of your hard disk is reserved for restore points. You can also delete all previous restore points. This is worth doing if – and only if – you have just removed a virus. That's because the virus could still be hiding in a restore point and you could reintroduce it by restoring your computer. In normal circumstances, you won't have any need to change the settings here.

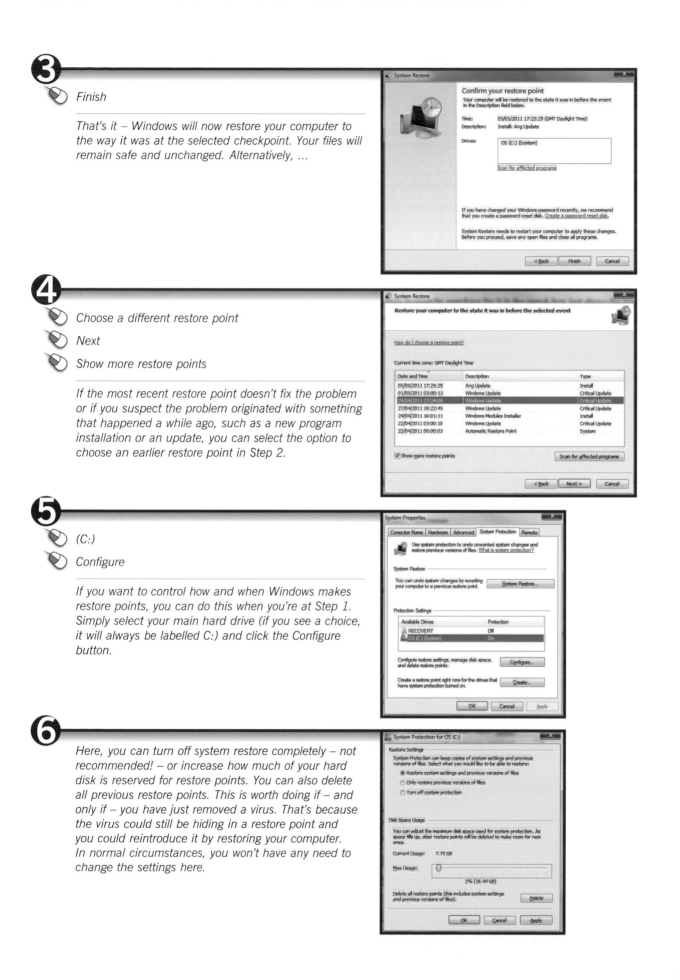

PART 5 Appendix 2 User accounts

Windows is customisable in all manner of ways, from the background picture on your Desktop to the colours used on screen and the way files and folders are displayed. With user accounts, it's even possible to set up a single computer to look and behave quite differently depending upon who's using it at the time. Stuffy dad may want a business-orientated machine with a minimum of frills and distractions; teenage son may prefer a Britney background and a focus on high-speed internet gaming; studious daughter may wish to ensure that her research files are not accidentally deleted by her careless brother (and perhaps keep him away from her private diary). User accounts let each member of the family arrange things entirely to their own suiting without affecting how others use the computer. What's more, each user account is protected with a password so the kids can't muck up dad's settings (and, to some extent, vice versa).

One for all the family

There are two levels of user account: *Administrator*, where the user can make system-wide changes, including installing and uninstalling programs; and *Standard user*, where the user can make changes to his or her own account but not interfere with the computer's main settings. We'll assume in the following example that you are the Administrator. Let's now set up a Standard user account for Jack, your imaginary son.

1

Start

Control Panel

User Accounts and Family Safety

Add or remove user accounts

You'll find User Accounts in the Control Panel. Here, we want to create a new account for Jack.

Create a new account

You may see a Guest account here. A Guest account is useful if you want people to be able to use your computer without requiring a full-blown account. However, we want to create an account, so click the link.

Jack

Standard user

Create Account

Give the new account a name and ensure that the Standard user button is selected. When you click Create Account, Windows will set up an account for Jack. When you next restart your computer, you will have a choice between your own account and Jack's.

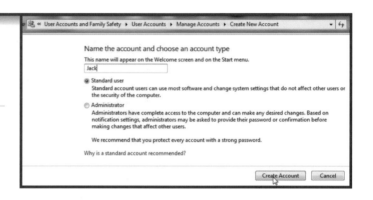

Start

Switch user

You can also switch between accounts from the Start button without restarting. It's perfectly possible to have two or more accounts open at the same time and switch between them at will. Each account is essentially personal to that user and can be configured however they like without affecting other users.

Administrator account

Change the account name

Return to Step 2 and click the Administrator account. Ours is rather unhelpfully named 'dell'. Let's make some changes.

6

TYPE *New name*

Change Name

It's easy to rename your default account like this. Using the options in Step 5, you can also change the picture (which appears at the top of the Start menu when you're logged in, as well as the login screen when you restart or switch users) and add or change a password.

7

Manage another account

Jack

Set up Parental Controls

On

Windows 7 has parental controls built in, which means you, with your Administrator account, can control how Jack, with his Standard user account, uses the computer. Just select his account and turn on the controls.

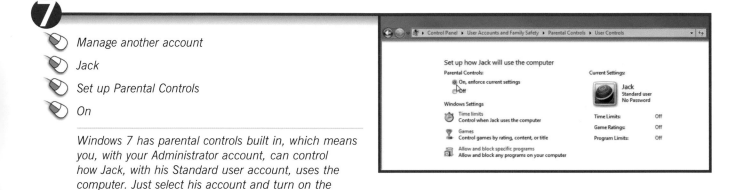

8

Time Limits

You can, for instance, prevent Jack from using the computer at all except during certain hours and even prevent access to certain games and programs. You can buy third-party software with many more options but Windows 7's own parental controls are simple and effective.

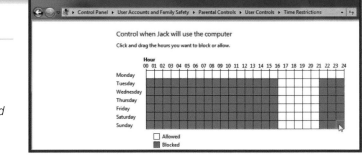

PART 5 Appendix 3 Using the Windows Action Center

Windows 7's Action Center (formerly known as the Windows Security Center) isn't just a sign that Microsoft can't be bothered changing American spellings to British ones: it's a one-stop shop for all your security needs.

To open Windows Action Center:

👆 *Start*

👆 *Control Panel*

👆 *System and Security*

👆 *Action Center*

1

Action Center will tell you about anything it thinks is a security risk. For example, in this screenshot, it isn't happy that we haven't set up Windows Backup. It knows about more than just backups, though. Click on the arrow to the far right of Security to see what's available.

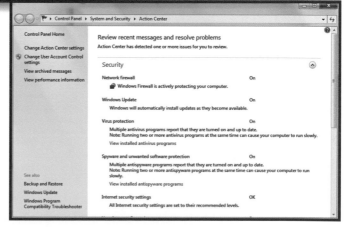

2

Action Center monitors several key things:

- *Windows Firewall prevents other computers from connecting to yours and also stops software connecting to the internet without your permission*
- *Windows Update automatically downloads the latest software updates and security fixes*
- *Spyware protection looks out for software that might be spying on you*
- *internet security settings control security on the internet*
- *User Account Control asks your permission before letting any program make changes to your system*
- *Network Access Protection is used by administrators of corporate networks.*

If any of these settings aren't to Action Center's satisfaction, it will warn you by displaying a flag in the Windows Taskbar, near the clock.

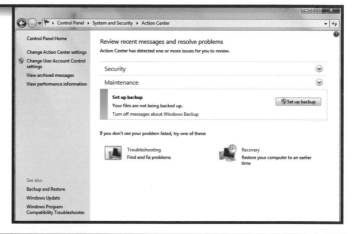

Using the Windows Firewall

Every PC has a number of ports, which are rather like doors in a building. E-mail might travel through one port, web pages through another, chat software through yet another and so on. Unfortunately many forms of dodgy software are actively looking for open ports that they can use to compromise your computer. At the same time, if there's malware on your computer it could be using those ports to surreptitiously phone home and transfer data about you. The Windows Firewall is designed to stop both kinds of connection.

For all its technology, the idea behind the Firewall is pretty simple: it goes around closing the doors that you're not currently using and, depending on how you set it, it either blocks any attempt to open more doors, or asks you what to do when it hears someone knocking.

To have a look at your Firewall settings:

Start

Control Panel

System and Security

Windows Firewall

Here you can see what is and isn't blocked – in our screenshot, we're blocking all connections to programs that aren't on our list of approved programs. You can change the settings by clicking the Advanced Settings link on the left of the window. You can also turn the Firewall off altogether, although we wouldn't recommend it.

One useful Windows Firewall feature is its ability to have different settings for different places, so for example you might have one set of firewall rules for when you're on your home network and a completely different, much more strict collection of rules for when you're connecting to public Wi-Fi hotspots.

Using Windows Update

Windows Update is an excellent thing: it automatically downloads Windows software updates and security fixes whenever they're released. You can run it manually whenever you like by clicking Start > All Programs > Windows Update. If you're connected to the internet, Windows Update will then see what's available. If you click on Change Settings, you'll see a range of options including the time of day when Windows Update should check for new updates and you can also change the automatic updating to manual or switch it off altogether. We'd advise against that, though, as that could potentially leave your PC unprotected against new nasties.

If you stick with the recommended settings you rarely need to do anything. From time to time a notification will pop up to tell you that Windows is installing new updates and occasionally you'll then see a pop-up informing you that you'll need to restart your computer to finish the installation process. That only tends to apply to really big updates, such as new versions of Internet Explorer, though. Most of the time, the updates will be installed without bothering or interrupting you.

It's worth occasionally running Windows Update manually even when it's set to install updates automatically, because there are two kinds of update: critical ones, which the automatic update process will install, and optional ones, which it won't. Optional updates can be all kinds of things, such as new language packs, updates to your video card software, or anything else Microsoft hasn't flagged as urgent.

Windows Update records the updates it installs on your PC. It doesn't take long before that's a very, very long list. It doesn't just look for updates to Windows itself, but to key programs such as your video card's software too.

◀ ▶ ▾ 🔍 ▸ Control Panel ▸ System and Security ▸ Windows Update ▸ View update history   ▾ | ✦

Review your update history

Check the Status column to ensure all important updates were successful. To remove an update, see Installed Updates.
Troubleshoot problems with installing updates

Name	Status	Importance	Date Installed
Definition Update for Microsoft Security Essentials - KB2310138 (Definition 1.103.408.0)	Successful	Optional	25/04/2011
Update for Microsoft Silverlight (KB2526954)	Successful	Important	25/04/2011
Update for Windows Live Essentials 2011 (KB 2520039)	Successful	Recommended	25/04/2011
Definition Update for Microsoft Security Essentials - KB2310138 (Definition 1.103.286.0)	Successful	Optional	22/04/2011
Security Update for Microsoft Visual C++ 2008 Service Pack 1 Redistributable Package (KB2467174)	Successful	Important	22/04/2011
nVidia - Display, Other hardware - NVIDIA GeForce 8200	Canceled	Optional	22/04/2011
Cumulative Security Update for ActiveX Killbits for Windows 7 for x64-based Systems (KB2508272)	Successful	Important	14/04/2011
Update for Windows 7 for x64-based Systems (KB2511250)	Successful	Recommended	14/04/2011
Security Update for Windows 7 for x64-based Systems (KB2506223)	Successful	Important	14/04/2011
Security Update for Windows 7 for x64-based Systems (KB2506212)	Successful	Important	14/04/2011
Security Update for Windows 7 for x64-based Systems (KB2508429)	Successful	Important	14/04/2011
Security Update for Windows 7 for x64-based Systems (KB2507618)	Successful	Important	14/04/2011
Security Update for Windows 7 for x64-based Systems (KB2509553)	Successful	Important	14/04/2011
Security Update for Windows 7 for x64-based Systems (KB2503658)	Successful	Important	14/04/2011
Update for Windows 7 for x64-based Systems (KB2506014)	Successful	Important	14/04/2011
Security Update for .NET Framework 3.5.1 on Windows 7 and Windows Server 2008 R2 SP1 for x64-based...	Successful	Important	14/04/2011
Windows Malicious Software Removal Tool x64 - April 2011 (KB890830)	Successful	Important	14/04/2011
Security Update for Windows 7 for x64-based Systems (KB2491683)	Successful	Important	14/04/2011

OK

Not all updates are installed automatically. To install optional updates, run Windows Update as normal by clicking Start > All Programs > Windows Update and then click on the bit where it says 'X optional updates are available', where X is the number of available updates.

You'll now see a list of available updates. In this example, there's an update to the display drivers for our video card. To install the update, we simply click on the appropriate tick box to select that update and then click on OK. If there's a big white exclamation mark in a blue circle when you click on an available update, that means you'll probably need to restart your PC to complete the installation process.

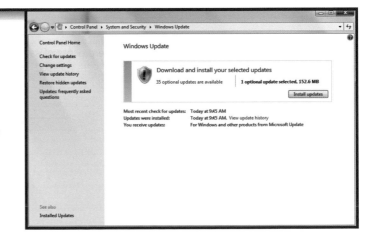

When you click on OK, you'll be returned to the main Windows Update window. To the right, you'll see how many updates you've selected to install and how big the download will be. Clicking on Install Updates will download and install the selected updates. Watch those download sizes: this single update is a mighty 152.6MB, which will take hours on a dial-up connection. If you're not on broadband, you may have to download some updates overnight.

PART ⑤ Glossary

Here we explain some of the terms mentioned but not really explored in the main part of the manual.

4.1/5.1 When an audio signal is split into several discrete channels and played back over correctly positioned speakers, the listener feels literally surrounded by sound (hence the term surround sound). A 4.1 speaker system uses four satellite speakers (two stereo speakers to the front and two behind) plus a subwoofer. In a 5.1 system, there is an additional central channel/speaker devoted to spoken dialogue in movie soundtracks.

A 4.1 speaker set up for surround sound.

(a)

ADSL Asymmetric Digital Subscriber Line. A technology that converts an ordinary household telephone line into a broadband internet connection. You can download data faster than you can upload it (hence the asymmetry).

Analogue A signal that varies continuously over time. For example, when a person speaks, the sound wave is an analogue signal, varying smoothly as they talk. Think of the hands on a traditional clock.

(b)

Background A program that works in the background is not obvious to the user (i.e. it doesn't appear in a window).

Bad old days Before Windows came DOS, a text-based operating system for personal computers. DOS is a mystery to most of us. Praise be for that.

Examples of buttons

Binary data A computer stores information in a coded form that involves nothing but long strings of 1s and 0s (i.e. it uses the binary numbering system).

Button An element of a program designed to look like a button. You can point at and click buttons with the mouse, at which point something will happen.

(c)

Cable Broadband internet access is often available through the same fibre-optic cables used to bring television and telephone services to homes and businesses.

CD burning The process of saving files to a compact disc. Commercial CDs are pressed, much like vinyl records of old, but a computer drive uses a laser to burn a pattern onto the surface of the disc.

A recordable CD drive gives you better backup options – and makes audio CDs to boot.

CD-R CD-Recordable. Recordable CDs can be filled with files once and once only.

CD-ROM CD-Read-Only Memory. Files can be read *from* a CD-ROM disc but you cannot record, or save, files to the disc.

CD-RW CD-ReWriteable. Rewriteable CDs can be filled with files repeatedly. Old files can be deleted to make space for new ones.

Check To check an option is to turn a particular feature on. To uncheck it is to turn that feature off.

Copy To copy a file is to create an exact digital duplicate of it without in any way affecting the original file.

CRT Cathode Ray Tube. A glass tube used to produce an image on some television sets and some computer monitors.

Data Any bit or collection of information used by or stored on a computer.

Default In the context of computing, a default option is selected automatically. For instance, a printer might print in draft mode by default. The use of 'default' implies that an alternative is available.

Delete To delete a file is to remove all record of it from a hard disk or other storage media. In practice, deleted files are not physically removed until some fresh file is allocated to the same disk space. This is why deleted files can often be 'magically' recovered.

Diagnostic utility A program that attempts to find and resolve problems with your computer.

A CRT monitor.

Dialogue box A window used by Windows to proffer information, offer choices and invite responses.

Dial-up An internet connection that relies upon a modem making a successful data call to an ISP over a telephone line.

Digital In contrast to analogue, a digital signal is composed of discrete packets of information (i.e. it moves sharply between fixed values). In terms of data, the digital data that your computer works with is 'simply' a string of 1s and 0s.

Disc/disk Disc is used with reference to *optical* storage media, such as a compact disc, and disk with reference to *magnetic* media, as in a floppy or hard disk.

An external modem.

Domain The top-level name of a website.

Download To download something is to transfer a copy of it from one computer to your own, especially but not exclusively across the internet.

DVD drive A DVD drive with the right software, video card and sound card can play DVD movies on a computer.

DVI Digital Visual Interface. A standard used to connect digital monitors to computers. A digital monitor can broadcast the pure digital signal generated by the computer's video card, with a resultant improvement in quality over that of analogue monitors, where the signal must first be converted from digital to analogue.

End user agreement See User licence.

Ethernet A high-speed standard used to connect computers with cables in a network.

Forum Discussion group contained within a website. All you need to take part is a browser.

Gigabyte A measure of data size. One gigabyte is 1,024 *megabytes*.

Hacker Somebody with the ability or aspiration to break into your computer through the internet, illegally.

Help menu In the context of a program, this is a (usually) searchable index of common questions and answers. If you get stuck, look for a Help button on the program Toolbar.

Hyperlink An element on a web page that, if clicked, opens another web page in your browser.

Icon A small image used by Windows to identify a file or program.

Instant chat/instant messenger An instant messenger program lets you conduct real-time two-way text conversations (called chat) across the internet. Windows comes with its own instant messenger – look in All Programs for Windows Messenger.

Interface In the context of software, the 'look and feel' of a program, such as its buttons, menus and windows. In hardware terms, it usually refers to a physical connection, like the USB interface.

Kilobyte A measure of data size. One kilobyte is 1024 bytes (and one byte is 8 bits).

LCD Liquid Crystal Display. A technology used to create flat-screen monitors that are much slimmer and lighter than CRT monitors.

Megabyte A measure of data size. One megabyte is 1,024 *kilobytes*.

Memory Memory is used to describe physical storage areas in a computer (i.e. places where data is saved). This includes Random Access Memory (RAM), which a computer uses as a temporary storage area. While you work on a letter with a word processor program, for example, the letter is 'held in RAM', and will be lost if the computer is turned off. If you save that letter, however, the file is allocated a chunk of hard disk space – another type of memory – and can be retrieved at any time.

Menu In the context of computers, a list of options from which you make a selection.

Modem A device that allows two computers to communicate with each other over a telephone line.

Motherboard The main circuit board inside a computer. Every other component connects to and communicates through the motherboard.

Network Any two or more computers connected together equals a network. They can be connected with cables, wirelessly, directly, or remotely. The internet is, of course, the grand-daddy of networks.

Don't forget to install a software player if you want to watch movies on your computer.

There's no getting away from it: LCD monitors are infinitely sleeker and sexier than their CRT cousins.

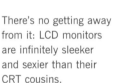

Online shopping You can buy stuff from virtual shops, like Amazon.com, over the internet. You can even have your groceries delivered to your door.

Overtype To overtype is to replace old text with new text without deleting the old text first. You can generally do this when the old text is highlighted.

Parallel port A single socket on the back of a computer typically used to connect a printer (before USB took over).

Parental controls Any software measure that lets somebody control, limit, supervise or otherwise modify the way somebody else uses a computer, particularly with regard to the internet.

Pop-up A menu that just 'pops up' on screen.

Processor A silicon chip that processes data very, very quickly. Effectively, the brain of your computer.

Restart To restart a computer is to turn it off and on again immediately.

Router A device that connects a PC to the internet.

Select To select something is, generally speaking, to click it. Once selected, an object becomes active (i.e. the focus of current activity).

Serial ports

Serial A pair (usually) of ports on the back of a computer once used to connect devices like mice and modems, but now increasingly obsolete.

Server A computer that is linked, directly or indirectly, to other computers and can be accessed by them. Servers are commonly used for large-scale data storage. The web consists of thousands of servers on which web pages are stored.

Session In computer-speak, a session is a period spent doing something or other. An internet session is a period spent online, for example.

Sound card An expansion card that lets a computer make sounds (providing there are speakers attached), particularly useful for playing music and games.

Streaming Streaming sound and video files are downloaded to your computer piece by piece. This means that you can start listening or watching them without having to wait for the whole file to download first.

Subwoofer A speaker designed to broadcast very low frequencies. An integral part of a surround sound system.

Surfing To surf is to visit web pages and click on links.

Surround sound See 4.1/5.1.

A sound card.

Technical support Virtually all ISPs offer some form of technical support by telephone by which you can call them up to seek assistance. This is often charged at premium rates, however. In many cases, you'll find that the ISP's customers are only too happy to pool resources and offer advice for free, often in newsgroups (see the entry above).

TWAIN A standard that get scanners talking to and working with programs. It's not an acronym, unfortunately, although urban legend insists it was coined for Technology Without An Interesting Name (we're happy to keep the myth alive).

USB Universal Serial Bus. A fast interface with which peripherals can connect to a computer. The beauty of USB is that it's hot-swappable, which means you can unplug one device and plug in another without restarting Windows. Now in its second, much faster incarnation, called USB 2.0.

User licence The terms and conditions governing ownership and use of a software program. Read a user licence once, just for kicks.

VGA Video Graphics Array. The most basic standard governing a video card's output and a monitor's display capability. Also used to describe the hardware connection between the card and monitor.

Video card An expansion card that lets a computer generate images on a monitor.

Web page A document stored on an internet server that can be viewed by anyone with an internet connection and a browser.

Web-based e-mail An e-mail service where you send and collect messages through your browser. Because web-based e-mail is independent of ISPs (i.e. it doesn't matter how you happen to be connected to the internet at the time) it is ideal for sending and picking up messages from anywhere in the world, particularly when travelling.

USB connectors.

A RAM module.

Index

ACKNOWLEDGEMENTS

Author	**Kyle MacRae**
Project Manager	**Louise McIntyre**
Design and page build	**James Robertson**
Copy editor and index	**Shena M Deuchars**
Photography	**Tom Bain**
Illustrations	**Matthew Marke**